DEATH

— *in* —

NEW YORK

DEATH

in

NEW YORK

HISTORY AND CULTURE OF
Burials, Undertakers & Executions

K. KROMBIE

THE
History
PRESS

Published by The History Press
Charleston, SC
www.historypress.com

All images are author's own unless otherwise noted.

First published 2021

Manufactured in the United States

ISBN 9781467149655

Library of Congress Control Number: 2021943809

Notice: The information in this book is true and complete to the best of our knowledge. It is offered without guarantee on the part of the author or The History Press. The author and The History Press disclaim all liability in connection with the use of this book.

CONTENTS

ACKNOWLEDGEMENTS

Thank you to two invaluable websites and their creators and contributors: findagrave.com, without which I would have been lost in a sea of headstones and sometimes taciturn cemetery offices, and the brilliant New York City Cemetery Project (https://nycemetery.wordpress.com), curated by Mary French, which I found myself studying long before the idea for this book fixed itself in my head. I highly recommend both websites for anyone interested in history and coordinates. Thanks most of all to Joshua Caleb Wright, for his bloodhound nose for tombstones, his thorough and thoughtful feedback on early drafts and his astounding interest in the baffling details of death in New York.

INTRODUCTION

In mid-nineteenth-century New York, burying the dead, a previously somber duty on the regular to-do list of a church sexton, became a business opportunity with far-reaching possibilities. On April 27, 1847, motivated by New York City's epidemics, overcrowding, fetid graveyards and burial prohibitions, the New York legislature passed "An act authorizing the incorporation of rural cemetery associations."

The commercial reach enabled by the act extended in all directions, the most significant of which was a patchwork of lands in Kings and Queens Counties on Long Island. Collectively, it was a rural landscape half a century away from entering the broad-shouldered huddle of New York City consolidation. Under the act, each burial ground could take up no more than 200 acres (amended to 250 acres by 1887) in one county, and so a number of cunning business heads banged together in order to overlap the border of two counties and potentially double their acres and income with tax-exempt real estate. Today, the unofficial name for the disorderly stretch of graves, tombs, crypts and columbariums in the boroughs of Brooklyn and Queens is the "Cemetery Belt." It is surrounded by a hinterland of forbidding freeways, drive-throughs, a few diffident neighborhoods and, fittingly, little human life. The Cemetery Belt features range from grandiose mausoleums, Gothic Revival architecture and pristine ornamentation to hollow tin grave markers, caved-in earth, fallen headstones and flagrant graffiti. In some of the worst cases, the inadequate maintenance is tied to a lack of funding from ever-decreasing

Manhattan skyline as seen from Calvary Cemetery.

descendants. In other instances, profiteering forces are impervious to benevolent supervision, but even the decaying areas possess a run-down consumptive beauty.

At the other end of the spectrum, throughout New York City, an astounding number of landmarks and seemingly unassuming neighborhood parks and playgrounds cover a multitude of forgotten generations still buried underneath. The burial grounds of the five boroughs tell the story of the city in increments, and as is typical for New York, they appear in episodic scene-stealing fashion: the skills and labor of enslaved people and immigrants who adapted and contributed to the city's foundations, the passing of state and city laws, the advancement of forensic science and sanitation, the phases of generational and economic development and the odyssey of the dead from churchyards and miscellaneous pits to commercial real estate and ever-evolving funerary options. In short, they represent the shape of a city.

I

THE OLDEST GRAVES AND ARTIFACTS

In 1897, Robert Peary, the Arctic explorer and the first person, by his own disputable claims, to reach the North Pole, brought six Inuit from Greenland to New York City aboard a ship called the *Hope*. The delivery of the Greenland six happened in response to the American Museum of Natural History's newly appointed assistant curator of ethnology and "Father of American Anthropology" Franz Boas's request for one Polar Inuk. From Inuit graves, Peary plucked human remains as additional research items for the museum. Understandably, the six Inuit were not happy about this, but Peary, whose previous 1895 expedition had resulted in thirty-seven Inuit deaths from an epidemic brought by his crew, promised the six that each of them would be back home within the year and given a stack of compensatory goods such as weapons and building materials.

Within months of the Inuit being quartered in the American Museum of Natural History's basement, during which time they were summoned as living specimens to be looked at and prodded and their measurements logged, the multilayered grime of city life seeped into their pitiful circumstances with fatal results. Two men, Qisuk and Nuktaq; Nuktaq's wife, Atangana; and their daughter, Aviaq, died of tuberculosis, while a third man, Uisaakassak, survived and was able to return to Greenland. Only one of the six remained, Qisuk's son, a boy of around seven called Minik, who was taken in by the family of William Wallace, the museum's superintendent of buildings.

The museum organized a funeral for Qisuk in the garden to satisfy his son, but unbeknownst to Minik, the body being lowered into the ground was in fact an effigy, a masked log wrapped in cloth. His father's body was actually at Bellevue Hospital's facility for Columbia University College of Physicians and Surgeons being de-fleshed and dissected for further study. The bones were then cleaned by Wallace, Minik's foster father, at his summer house property. Nuktaq, Atangana and Aviaq befell the same fate as Qisuk, and the remains of all four became the possessions of the Osteological Department of the American Museum of Natural History. Minik discovered what had happened a

Minik Wallace. *Public domain.*

decade later when a newspaper exposé revealed the truth about the fake burial. Wallace confirmed that Minik, who claimed later to have seen his father's skeleton on display at the museum, was never the same again. The fact that the museum has maintained that the Inuit bodies were never exhibited doesn't quite lessen the blow of this miserable episode.

Minik's pleas to have his father's body returned to his homeland were ignored by the museum but highly publicized in the nation's press. Following bouts of depression and pneumonia, Minik was at last able to return to Greenland in 1909. After relearning his original language, he worked sporadically over the next several years as a translator and guide. Unable to fully assimilate due to spending so many years in New York, Minik came back to America in 1916 and drifted to New Hampshire the following year. He found work as a lumberjack but succumbed to the flu epidemic of 1918. Minik died of pneumonia on October 29, 1918, and was buried at Indian Stream Cemetery in Pittsburg, New Hampshire.

In 1993, the remains of Minik's father and the three other Inuit were shipped back to Greenland by the American Museum of Natural History. Almost a century after their deaths in New York City, and thanks to Kenn Harper reviving Minik's story in his 1986 book, *Give Me My Father's Body: The Life of Minik, the New York Eskimo* (an updated version, *Minik: The New York Eskimo*, was published in 2017), Qisuk, Nuktaq, Atangana and Aviaq were given traditional burial rites.

A few years later, in 1998, Bill Stevens, the owner of Evolution, a Manhattan SoHo boutique that specialized (at that time) in transporting and selling the remains of endangered animals, human fetuses and the skulls of Seminole and Peoria tribespeople, was sentenced to ninety days in jail and ordered to pay a $10,000 fine.

Historically, the relationship between cabinets of curiosity and ethnographic museums with indigenous peoples has been far from civil. Credible and persuasive accusations of theft, exploitation and misinterpretation have a habit of sullying the display cases. Meanwhile, countless human dead, together with burial keepsakes turned spoils, have been dug up and carted off from all regions and eras to be exhibited for the greater good that is our cumulative education. The rationale behind old-fashioned museum plunder proposes that for every unimpressed despondent child on a museum field trip, there will be another in that same group who might look at an exhibit, read the accompanying text and learn just enough to partially justify the checkered past of indigenous acquisitions, and so, figuratively at least, all is not lost.

The archaeological acquisitions of a number of New York museums have, of course, come from the city's own soil. While some historians believe that the island of Manhattan was inhabited only seasonally and used mostly as a hunting station—which along with the discovery of weaponry, tools, wampum, shell heaps and canoes would explain the absence of substantial Lenape burial grounds—contemporary accounts from the Dutch West India Company's trading post of New Amsterdam (declared an official city in 1653) clearly indicate that indigenous occupancy, though often transitory in accordance with seasonal food sources and hunting opportunities, was perpetually present. While there is historical and archaeological evidence of the Lenape living in settlements or villages on the southern part of the island as well as the north, including Sapokanikan in today's Greenwich Village and Nechtanc at Corlears Hook on the Lower East Side, significant burial sites have yet to present themselves. One explanation may be that casketless burials in shallow graves provide extra momentum for skeletal decomposition as the elements take over.

The Lenni-Lenape, or more commonly the Lenape, meaning "Original" or "Real People," belong to the Delaware Nation. Far from being an indigenous word, the Delaware state and river are named after Thomas West, the third Baron De La Warr and governor of the Virginia Colony, who, for the record, never visited his namesake. The Lenape lived in relatively small, scattered groups with distinct dialects and customs in longhouses and roundhouses called wigwams. Their population in the regions that would become the five boroughs of New York City may have been as large as fifteen thousand by the time the Dutch company town of New Amsterdam began to lay its foundations in the 1620s. Long before the white man arrived, the Lenape's sophisticated trade routes and communication network extended far and wide. Their prime medium of exchange was wampum, beaded shells that were one of the main currencies traded throughout the early Dutch and British colonies.

All things considered, the Lenape were considerably generous and accommodating to those pioneers who arrived looking to move into and make capital out of the New World, where the Lenape had been living, relatively undisturbed for approximately three thousand years. The first wave of Paleo-Indian habitation of the New York City area occurred nine to twelve thousand years ago following migration from Asia via the Beringia land bridge between Alaska and Siberia. Finding human remains from this period, thus far in Alaska and Idaho, is extremely rare.

The Lenape territory, Lenapehoking, stretched from western Connecticut to eastern Pennsylvania and the Hudson Valley to Delaware. Manhattan comes from the Lenape word *Manahatta*, believed to mean "hilly (or small) island." Many indigenous words were likely to have been misconstrued, mispronounced or repurposed to mean a language, such as Munsee, a subgroup of the Algonquian language spoken mainly in the Manhattan area, or place names like Carnarsie in Brooklyn and Jamaica in Queens. Mahicantuck and Shatemuc are among a number of Lenape words for the Hudson River, meaning "great waters in constant motion" and "the river that flows both ways," respectively—two accurate descriptions of the ways of the estuary.

The Wecquaesgeek were a band of the Wappinger people, a branch of the Lenape who mixed and made alliances with the Mohicans to the north. The Wecquaesgeek not only inhabited the land just north of the city in what is today Westchester County, trickling down through the Bronx and the top of Manhattan, but they also had the controlling upper hand on the island of Manhattan. Consequently, Wickquasgeck was the name of a prominent trail that led northward from the southern tip of Manhattan Island. Today, the southern part of that original trail is the major thoroughfare, Broadway.

When Peter Minuit, a Walloon—raised in Germany—acting on behalf of the chartered Dutch West India Company (formed in 1621 to develop trading posts in North America, Brazil, the Caribbean and Africa), purchased Manhattan Island in 1626 in exchange for goods that were valued at sixty guilders, the indigenous people and the Dutch had vastly different concepts of land ownership. In addition, there was no cash exchange; the goods exchanged may have been equal to that amount, but the amount was immaterial to the goods that were to be gained. For the Lenape, land, and that which grew on it, as well as the passing of the seasons and the changing of the weather, were but elements of an interactive environment that convened and cooperated according to the instinctive order of the natural world. Such a thing as land could not be owned, only inhabited, and so for the Lenape, the transaction more than likely represented their consent for the land to be shared.

Early European settlers described the Lenape as fit and attractive and, in the warmer months, naked from the waist up. Skin paint and feathers decorated bodies that were partially covered in animal skins and furs. They were matrilineal; the bloodline of women determined who their leaders would be. Turkey, Turtle and Wolf made up the three main Lenape clans. Sons paired up with women from other clans, and any offspring belonged to the clan of their maternal grandmother.

There were noteworthy periods when the colonists of New Netherland (which extended westward and southward from Connecticut to New York, New Jersey, Delaware and Pennsylvania), noted for their tolerance, leniency and ethnic diversity when compared with the Puritan colonies of northern New England, lived in peace with the indigenous people, whom they relied on for trade. The average Lenape person's lifespan was relatively short at around thirty to forty years. This was the reason for their youthful nuptials and a consequence of living in an often-harsh, demanding environment. Then came the diseases shipped from Europe, among them, smallpox and influenza, to which the immune systems of indigenous people had no resistance. Throughout the colonized areas of North America, indigenous people were wiped out at an estimated rate of up to 90 percent in the first one hundred years of European settlement.

Naturally, they defended themselves when the mounting European colonists demonstrated their commitment to seizing land and decimating their existence, such as the massacre of five to seven hundred individuals of a multi-tribal gathering that included the Lenape at Westchester's Pound Ridge at the command of an Englishman, Captain John Underhill, on behalf of Director of New Netherland Willem Kieft. (Underhill, who also happens to be an ancestor of Amelia Earhart, Tom Selleck and Johnny Depp, is name-checked on a Daughters of the American Revolution "Kings Highway" plaque at Brooklyn's Flatlands Dutch Reformed Churchyard just for having passed through.) The combination of multiple pandemics; conflict over land that was transformed and flattened through developmental change; and the weight of the competitive fur trade, made gargantuan by European gluttony for felt hats, took its toll. The resulting Lenape diaspora took the larger part of the few who were left as far as Oklahoma, Wisconsin and Ontario.

Long after American independence, when the Lenape were all but gone from the New York City area, the new American cathedral-like museums were nourished by competitive archaeological fervor. The Manhattan area of Inwood, having changed its name from the much more jovial Tubby Hook in the mid-nineteenth century, became ripe for archaeological investigation.

The almost two-hundred-acre Inwood Hill Park, which curls around the Hudson River and Spuyten Duyvil (Devil's Spout) Creek up to the northern tip of Manhattan, is the last remaining remnant of the island's precolonial natural topography. Aside from Revolutionary meddling by the Continental and British armies at Fort Cockhill at the hill's northwesterly peak, the odd summer mansion and wintry institution (since demolished) and the footpaths that appeared courtesy of the New Deal's National Youth Administration in the 1930s, the area has been largely untampered with. Burrowed inside the only natural forest in Manhattan in a vicinity that includes the oldest glacial pothole in the city, an active fault line, Inwood marble and the last remaining salt marsh in Manhattan, are the "Indian caves"—more precisely, schist protrusions—in a steep rough-and-tumble configuration, deposited by Upper Paleolithic rockfall. Each of these shelter caves were used by the indigenous people of New York as part of a larger seasonal camp called Shorakkopoch, for storage, cooking and habitation.

During the late nineteenth and early twentieth centuries, Inwood's preserved natural history, surviving pre-European trade route (today's Indian Road) and the new real estate and subway extension engineering developments provided an in for curious minds. Three engineers, Alexander Chenoweth, William Louis Calver, and Reginald Pelham Bolton, each of them enthusiastic amateur historians and archaeologists, acted on their shared interests by exploring Inwood's hidden layers. As a result of their amateur research, two of them, Calver and Bolton, were selected by the New York Historical Society to continue their work as part of the museum's field committee, with Calver as its chairman.

In 1890, Chenoweth, a prominent society figure and chief engineer of the Croton Aqueduct, began an excavation of the Inwood caves. Inside, he uncovered shell heaps—an indication of a refuse stack or pit—and a treasure-trove of priceless Lenape artifacts: pottery pieces and arrow and

Indian Caves of Inwood Hill Park.

axe heads beneath the soil and in larger inner chambers. Public opinion was divided over his activities, with the worst of it opposed to what was perceived to be the desecration of a sacred site. Chenoweth would go on to sell his collection to the American Museum of Natural History. At a place called the Knoll, also in Inwood, he found skeletons buried beneath rugged headstones. Contrary to what Chenoweth and the contemporary press reports claimed, in scientific circles the skeletons were believed to be the remains of early colonists.

The skeleton of a baby mastodon, not the first of its kind to be found in the New York City area, was happened upon at Dyckman Street by baffled construction workers in 1925, shortly before one of its giant teeth was snatched away by an opportunistic milkman who happened to be passing by. About a dozen dead dogs covered with shells were discovered within the same general area, two within fifty yards of each other near the Harlem River. Calver deduced that they were part of a Lenape sacrificial ceremony, not unlike the midwinter ceremony, the White Dog Sacrifice, of the Iroquois of Upstate New York, in which white dogs were asphyxiated, decked out with wampum and then burned with the aim of sending them off as messengers to the great Creator. Another more palatable reason for their frequency could be that they were valued animals, trained by the Lenape and considered to have unique access into the spiritual realm.

In August 1907, beneath a local garden, Bolton—a competitive foe of Chenoweth's as well as the savior of notable historic New York houses that would otherwise have been demolished (Poe Cottage, Dyckman Farmhouse)—dug up an intact human skeleton on a protective bed of oyster shells, flexed in "Indian fashion," that is, in a fetal-like position with the arms and legs bent toward the body.

The following year, near the Revolutionary relics of Fort Cockhill's campfire site, William Calver and an ethnologist, lecturer and scientific researcher for the American Museum of Natural History and later the Museum of the American Indian, Alanson Buck Skinner, discovered the intact skeleton of a grown man, also in the flexed position and, in front of it, the dismembered bones of a woman purposefully arranged in a rectangular bundle. In 1908, half a dozen meters north of the campfire site, another intact skeleton of a flexed elderly woman was found with the fragments of a small child between her knees. Skinner and Chenoweth went on to discover different parts of another skeleton close by, while the remains of a young woman were found by sewage workers on Seaman Avenue. None of the Inwood skeletons were buried with significant funeral items, but all were believed to be from the Late Woodland period, which ended with the arrival of Europeans.

Beyond Manhattan, in the counties that were consolidated into the five boroughs of New York City in 1898, evidence of indigenous burial sites is decidedly mixed. Excavations of Gerritsen's Creek in Brooklyn, at the southwesterly edge of Long Island in the Marine Park area of Jamaica Bay, have been occurring since 1997. The largest park in Brooklyn, Marine Park is of particular interest to historic and prehistoric researchers. European settlers were quick to populate the area soon after laying claim to Manhattan. The nearby Flatlands is believed to have been the center of the largest Lenape gathering site in Brooklyn. The area's indigenous name, Keshaechquern, had a central meetinghouse for the Canarsee, the Lenape branch of western Long Island. Multiple references have been made throughout its European-settled history of a Canarsee burial ground in the areas of Gerritsen's Creek and the Flatlands Dutch Reformed Church, but so far, while there have been significant archaeological discoveries, material evidence of the dead has not been forthcoming.

Elsewhere in the borough, the Brooklyn Historical Society is in possession of a 1946 map called *Indian Villages, Paths, Ponds and Places in Kings County*. It was drawn up by an Irishman, James Angelo Kelly, who had immigrated to Brooklyn from County Longford as a child before developing an impressive résumé. In his time, he had been a construction worker, soldier, teacher, singer/songwriter, deputy county clerk of Kings County and New York's first official borough historian. According to Kelly, the map marks the spot of a Lenape burial ground that has long since been covered up by the development of the Boerum Hill and Gowanus neighborhoods.

In 1931 in Little Neck, Queens, a cemetery used by the Matinecoc of Long Island was demolished by the widening of Northern Boulevard. Despite the protestations of Chief Wild Pigeon, around thirty bodies were reinterred at the nearby Zion Episcopal Churchyard in Douglaston. The burial transfer is believed to have left behind family members, while items they were buried with went missing. A split boulder inscribed with "Here rest the last of the Matinecoc" marks the reinterment ground. In January 2018, a little over two years after the area acknowledged its oldest residents by co-naming a local intersection Matinecock Way, Chief Harry Wallace of the Unkechaug Nation of Long Island led a homecoming ceremony at the churchyard's reinterment spot for the repatriated Matinecoc ancestral remains that were relocated from the Museum of Arts and Sciences in Daytona Beach, Florida.

In Robert Bolton's *A History of the County of Westchester*, published in 1848, he writes of numerous burial mounds on the shore of Pelham Bay along the northeastern part of the Bronx. Since the start of its construction in 1888, Van Cortlandt Park, to the west of Pelham Bay and the city's third-largest parkland, has been shaped and pruned around ancient woodland while playing the long game of hide and seek with a multitude of history. In 1890, amid substantial evidence of a former Wickquasgeck village known as Mosholu, thirteen intact skeletons, believed to be indigenous people, were removed during excavations of the Parade Ground on the west side of the park and promptly handed over to the American Museum of Natural History. On the east side of Van Cortlandt Park in a place called Indian Field, a cairn-style monument, erected by the Daughters of the American Revolution, pays tribute to Chief Nimham and his band of seventeen Mohicans, converts to Christianity who hailed from the mission village of Stockbridge, Massachusetts. Slain by Lieutenant Colonel John Graves Simcoe's British and Hessian soldiers on August 31, 1778, at the Battle of Kingsbridge, they were buried where they fell.

In 1934, just north of the city, Mrs. Allen Spink of Croton-on-Hudson in Westchester County was reasonably alarmed when she dug up a six-foot man while doing a spot of gardening. Evidence of a club to the head was the least interesting thing about the dead man under Mrs. Spink's spade. The nearby arrowheads, his broken right shin bone and physical evidence of him having once modeled the hairstyle consistent with a chief led researchers to believe that he was none other than Chief Mamaroneck, otherwise known as Limping Will, who "sold" the Croton area in the seventeenth century to European settlers. The bones were then handed over to the local historical society. In the ensuing decades, debates have ranged from whether Mamaroneck and Limping Will are in fact two different people, whether the bones belong to either one or to someone else entirely and whether they should be returned to the ground and buried.

Many of the inhabitants of pre-twentieth-century Staten Island, whose agricultural environment nestled from its western perimeter into the curve of mainland New Jersey, observed the arrowheads and hammerstones that frequently turned up in the lay of the land, leftovers from the Raritan, the Staten Island branch of the Lenape. In 1903, at the Church of Ascension in West New Brighton, flexed skeletons were discovered in an area that already had burial ground continuity as a churchyard cemetery. In the same vicinity, residents claimed to have witnessed human bones seeping out from underneath sand dunes during heavy rain. In *The Indians of Greater New York and the Hudson*, published in 1909 as part of the *Anthropological Papers of the American Museum of Natural History*, Alanson Skinner describes significant indigenous burial grounds in several locations along the western shoreline. Each of these sites were surrounded by evidence of village-type habitation, settlement refuse, pottery fragments, tools, weaponry and animal bones.

During the first decade of the twentieth century at Mariner's Harbor, a team that included Skinner found a number of skeletons, many of them flexed, with some sharing a single grave space three or four feet beneath the sand and one belonging to an elderly woman buried with a baby lynx. The condition of further bone burials suggested that they were interred after the flesh had decomposed. Dutch navigator, merchant and patroon David De Vries, who established a settlement on Staten Island in 1639, and whose hogs, upon being stolen, set the ball rolling for the massacres of Kieft's War (fought between the hawkish New Netherland director William Kieft and the surrounding indigenous people), made reference in his journal to the Raritan keeping some of their dead in their homes and burying the bones at a later date, while others were buried soon after their death in graves lined with boughs and covered with clay.

In 1895, Staten Island local, ethnologist and archaeologist George Hubbard Pepper, working on behalf of the American Museum of Natural History after conducting his own independent research, dug up Staten Island's best-known burial ground at what is now known as Burial Ridge at Ward's Point Archaeological Site in Tottenville. The sandy bluffs of Burial Ridge form the rim of today's Conference House Park at the southernmost

Archaeological excavation of Burial Ridge in Ward's Point. *Public domain.*

point of New York State. Instances of human remains being professionally excavated, casually dug up or popping up uninvited, flexed, sitting and even one standing, have been recorded in the area since 1858. Among the otherwise peaceful burials, a discernible number evidently expired from violence, including a male skeleton scorched from the knees up, suggesting death by fire with intent; another with his skull deliberately caved in; and more than one shot through with antler and bone arrowheads. Many of the dead of Ward's Point were buried with jewelry and ornaments that set them apart from the Inwood burials. Burial Ridge is the largest indigenous grave site in all five boroughs and thus far the biggest peephole into the lives and deaths of pre-colonial New York.

Throughout the United States, the immense diversity of indigenous life and many nature-based religions have fostered a variety of funerary traditions, including burial in earth, caves, ravines and trees, with the dead sometimes wrapped in shawls and buried with personal belongings to take with them to the next plane of existence. Similarly, the precolonial burial traditions of the Lenape would have almost certainly diversified over their widespread region. For instance, in Daniel Denton's *A Brief Description of New York*, first published in 1670, he describes the burial ritual of a group of indigenous Long Islanders—already dwindling in numbers by the time he put pen to paper—thus:

> *When any Indian dies amongst them, they bury him upright, sitting upon a seat, with his Gun, money, and such goods he hath with him, that he may be*

Present-day Burial Ridge in Ward's Point, Staten Island.

furnished in the other world, which they conceive is Westward, where they shall have great store of Game for Hunting and live easie [sic] *lives. At his Burial his nearest Relations attend the Hearse with their faces painted black, and do visit the grave once or twice a day, where they send forth sad lamentations so long, till time hath worn the blackness of their faces, and afterwards every year once they view the grave, make a new mourning for him, trimming up the Grave, not suffering of a Grass to grow by it: they fence their graves with a hedge, and cover the tops with Mats, to shelter them from the rain.*

Preserving the history of indigenous New York burial customs has been difficult due to four centuries of displacement. However, uncovering burials in eastern North America on or near middens is not uncommon, and refuse stacks, often mixed with charcoal, have held together a common thread of indigenous death ritual. When the Lenape adopted the European tradition of using coffins, a small incision was cut into the top by the head so that the soul of the deceased could come and go.

Besides the history, arts and culture-promoting Lenape Center; the annual Pow Wows at Inwood Hill Park and Queens County Farm; and Tammany Hall's glass turtle shell roof (representing the turtle origin story as well as the Turtle Clan's chief and Penn's Treaty cosigner, Tamanend, after whom Tammany Hall and the Tammany Society were named), there are few reminders of the indigenous presence in New York City except for selected street and place names and, of course, the National Museum of the American Indian. The site of the present-day museum was once occupied by Fort Amsterdam, built in the mid-1620s to protect the Dutch colony from competitive European powers and any known or unknown quantity of indigenous combatants. It was renamed Fort James after the British takeover in 1664 and retitled a few more times before it was dismantled in 1790 by newly independent Americans.

Adding to the New York custom of engineers taking up amateur archaeology, electrical engineer George Gustav Heye set about collecting the largest collection of indigenous American artifacts in the world. Heye began his collection in 1903, and in 1922 he opened the Museum of the American Indian in Washington Heights. In Lower Manhattan, on the site of the old fort, the Cass Gilbert–designed Custom House parted ways with the United States Custom Service in the 1970s. In 1990, the building was renamed in honor of founding father and first secretary of the treasury Alexander Hamilton. Heye's collection was transferred to the Smithsonian Institution in 1989, and in 1994, the Alexander Hamilton U.S. Custom House reopened as the George Gustav Heye Center of the National Museum of the American Indian.

In 1906, President Theodore Roosevelt signed the Antiquities Act into law, authorizing the president of the United States to create national monuments from historic and prehistoric landmarks and structures. The act stipulated that any person found excavating or destroying monuments or objects of antiquity without permission could be fined or imprisoned. Almost a century later, the 1990 Native American Graves Protection and Repatriation Act required that federal agencies and museums receiving federal funds must attempt to reach agreements with Indian tribes and native Hawaiian organizations regarding the repatriation of human remains and objects. According to the National Museum of the American Indian, about twenty-five thousand items in its collection correspond with the five categories of eligible items for repatriation: human remains, funerary objects, sacred objects, objects of cultural patrimony and illegally acquired items. At the time of writing, the museum "retains fewer than three hundred catalogued human remains" and "has repatriated more than two thousand items."

2

BLOODSHED AND AMBITION

Probing the unknown is a risky business. The destinies of the first European visitors to the area that would become New York City were no exception. In 1524, in pursuit of the Northwest Passage trade route to Asia on behalf of King Francis I of France, Florentine explorer Giovanni da Verrazzano became the first European to discover New York Bay in addition to other key places along the Eastern Seaboard. Verrazzano's death occurred only four years later, and the route of it, according to the most popular version of his disappearance, was down the gullets of Caribbean cannibals on the island of Guadeloupe.

In 1525, Estêvão Gomes, a Portuguese navigator, also in pursuit of the Northwest Passage, this time on behalf of Spain, happened upon the same bay and a river that he called El Rio San Antonio. His exact route out and the breadth of his coverage of the Manhattan waterways are unknown. The resulting cartography of the American East Coast was nevertheless impressively accurate. What is known is that Gomes kidnapped dozens of indigenous people—possibly from Maine or Nova Scotia—who were then set free upon arrival in Spain by Charles V. In 1538, Gomes was killed by indigenous people in Paraguay.

In 1609, lured by that same elusive passage, a sixteen-man Dutch and English crew aboard the *Halve Maen* (*Half Moon*), led by Englishman Henry Hudson on behalf of the Dutch East India Company, sailed between the forest-covered hills and salt marshes of northeastern New Jersey and Manhattan, on the river that would one day take the name of the ship's

"Henry Hudson, the celebrated and unfortunate navigator, abandoned by his crew in Hudson's Bay the 11th of June 1610," drawn by F. Davignon. Incidentally, the mutiny actually occurred in 1611. *Public domain.*

captain, the same river that Gomes had called San Antonio. A few days into exploring this particular region of the North American continent and after exchanging gifts and pleasantries with the local Lenape, one of Hudson's men, John Colman, was shot in the neck by an arrow from an ambush of not-so-friendly locals in two canoes. The exact whereabouts of his hasty burial by the *Halve Maen* crew continues to be debated. Nevertheless, Colman's fate gifted him with the lonely accolade of being the first European to be killed and buried on the banks of New York Bay.

Spurred on by his discovery of new and advantageous land and waterways, Henry Hudson led a second North American voyage aboard the *Discovery* in 1610–11. This expedition, once again in search of that mysterious shortcut to international trade with the East (but this time funded by Hudson's fellow countrymen), stretched out through miserable icy conditions and a fruitless search. Angry mutineers, exasperated by their commander's rigid authority in such debilitating circumstances, forced Hudson and his teenage son into a small boat with several short straw crew members. Those set adrift were never to be seen again. The Canadian waters in which they were last seen by the departing mutineers would one day be called Hudson Bay.

Investing time and effort in New York City, even for those who have anchored in its waters momentarily, can be defined by the handheld pairing of bloodshed and ambition that have skipped and kicked through the city's history. The first wave of European settlers of New Amsterdam, nudged aboard vessels by the Dutch West India Company, whose goal was to populate the promising outpost born of Henry Hudson's discovery, were hardly sacrificial lambs. The company, which traded in far-flung goods and people, while wading in piracy and uncharted territory, was focused on profit, not the religious dogma or oppressive domesticity that was prevalent in so much of Europe.

The seventeenth-century settlers of New Amsterdam at the southern tip of Manhattan Island, which would soon become the commercial and social hub of the spread-eagling Dutch colony of New Netherland, sunned themselves in free trade, social diversity, slang and patois from the heady mix of nationalities and languages, stunning scenery, brothels, taverns and a fresh set of freedoms and ideas that grew out of the extraordinary new playground of their remote and fertile land. It is apt, then, that Saint Nicholas, the patron saint of repentant thieves and prostitutes (among other less egregious job descriptions), the blueprint for Santa Claus and the namesake of New Amsterdam's "Church in the Fort," is also the patron saint of New York City.

Life in the colony was marred too by the presence of slavery, pestilence, isolation and the perpetual fear of how the warring factions of Europe and the tit-for-tat massacres with the indigenous people of the surrounding lands could affect them at any moment. The narrow thirteen-mile-long island of Manhattan jutted out of a behemoth wilderness. The full-scale perimeters and landscapes of the North American continent were still unknown. From day to day, the colony was surrounded by immeasurable danger. The possibility of dying from any number of untreatable diseases, accidents, execution or murder was a hefty and carnivorous fact of everyday life.

It isn't hard to imagine that the growing number of patroons, burghers and self-made merchants cultivated their Manhattan farmsteads to include family burial grounds, the remains of which would be submerged in the years to come beneath the gleaming towers of the Manhattan skyline and the subterranean networks of sewers and train tunnels. There are numerous colonial and Early Republic–era family cemeteries acknowledged by the twenty-first century with mostly long-gone headstones in the outer boroughs such as the Bedell-Decker (Staten Island), Brinckerhoff, Remsen, Cornell, Pullis Farm, Thorne-Wilkins and Wyckoff-Snedike (Queens), Barkaloo (Brooklyn), and Ferris (Bronx) burial grounds.

Proportionate to the developing New Amsterdam population and for the duration of its forty years, just one official cemetery within the city walls was sufficient—or made the best of at any rate. Communal worship was towed toward Saint Nicholas Church, the Dutch Reformed Church at Fort Amsterdam, erected in 1642. Most other religions were begrudgingly tolerated due to the 1579 Union of Utrecht, signed by the United Provinces of the Netherlands during their fight for independence from Spain in the Eighty Years' War. One condition of the treaty—that "no other Province shall be permitted to interfere or make difficulties, provided that each person shall remain free in his religion and that no one shall be investigated or persecuted because of his religion"—etched the critical specification of modernity into the Dutch Republic and the American Republic two centuries later. Furthermore, the Holland-based officials behind the company town of New Amsterdam were understandably cautious about offending any religious faction that may have invested in the Dutch West India enterprise.

Director-General Peter Stuyvesant, the colony's last and longest-standing leader (albeit on one leg, his right having been amputated after getting crushed by a cannonball during a Dutch attack on the Spanish at Saint Martin in 1644), who was the son of a Calvinist minister and singular in both his managerial efficiency and narrow-mindedness, would have banished all religions but his had he not had to surrender to the will of his superiors in Amsterdam. He did, however, manage to provisionally succeed in kicking out the Quakers, who, having set down roots in neighboring Long Island, presented him with the Flushing Remonstrance, a forerunner of the First Amendment, in protest to his religious prohibition.

French Calvinists, otherwise known as Huguenots, were especially prevalent in numbers and influence in New Amsterdam, with Belgian Walloons among them. The official date for the founding of Manhattan's Huguenot Saint-Esprit congregation is Easter Sunday 1628. Today, it is an all-inclusive Episcopal church on the Upper East Side with French-language Sunday sermons. Saint-Esprit's second church, situated between today's Federal Hall and the Federal Reserve Bank of New York in the Financial District, was built in 1704 to replace a smaller church at Petticoat Lane. It stood for over a century with an adjoining graveyard, but in 1831, within a year of the *New York Mirror* declaring, "In a few more fleeting years not a single vestige of the original city will remain," the residents of the Saint-Esprit graveyard were moved when the church, pushed by the city's expansion, relocated farther north.

Some of the Saint-Esprit dead were transferred to a vault at Saint Mark's Church in-the-Bowery in today's East Village, at the same spot where Peter Stuyvesant was interred upon his death in 1672. After losing his colony to the English in 1664, Stuyvesant lived out his remaining years on his farm, his *bouwerie*, from which Bowery, one of Manhattan's oldest streets, gets its name. He was interred with the remains of his slaves in the family vault under what was then his own private Dutch Reformed chapel.

A longtime staple of East Village counterculture, Saint Mark's Church in-the-Bowery was built in 1799 by John McComb Jr. on the site of Peter Stuyvesant's chapel, making it the longest continuous site of worship in the city. Plotted and crafted by Stuyvesant's great-great-grandson, Saint Mark's was granted legal permission to practice independently of Trinity Church by Alexander Hamilton, who, in addition to his other prominent duties, happened to be Trinity's parish attorney. When the last of the Stuyvesants, Augustus Van Horne Stuyvesant, an unmarried recluse beholden to the confines of his Fifth Avenue mansion, died in 1953, a stipulation in his will was duly carried out. As soon as he was interred in the family vault, said to contain eighty members of the Stuyvesant family, it was filled in with concrete and forever sealed shut.

Translated from seventeenth-century Low Dutch, New Amsterdam's *Minutes of the Court of Burgomasters and Schepens 1656 to Aug, 27, 1658* is packed with squabbles over money and slander, including one case of a plaintiff demanding "surgeon fees" from the defendant, who struck him "with a thorn stick" after the plaintiff allegedly called him a "French bugger." On January 28, 1656, at Pearl Street's Stadt Huys (statehouse), the City Tavern turned City Hall, the records make mention of the city cemetery and its condition. Burgomaster Allard Anthony made the following proposition: "Whereas the [honorable] General has proposed to him that it is highly necessary to divide the Old Graveyard, which is wholly in ruins into lots to be built upon, and to make another Grave-Yard, south of the Fort, and to remove the houses standing there, in a valuation, what resolution shall be taken there upon?" It was decided that it was "highly necessary to establish a Graveyard at another suitable place, or to put it in good order where it now is."

The situation with the "Old Graveyard," visible on the Castello Plan (city map) of 1660 and positioned where Broadway meets Morris Street, is the first recorded instance of a New York City cemetery in terrible condition. It wouldn't be the last. Almost certainly, its "in ruins" state was down to the usual lack of municipal funding and a population boom. Between New Amsterdam's official beginning in 1625 and the British takeover in 1664

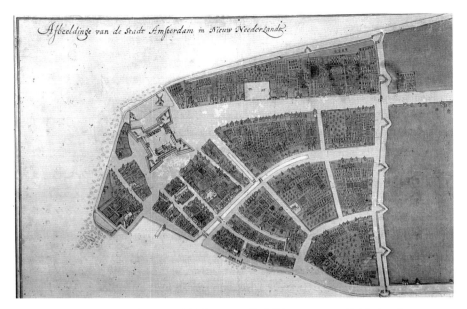

The 1660 Castello Plan, with the "Old Graveyard" visible top center. *Public domain.*

that renamed the city after the Duke of York (the future King James II of England), the city's population, not including the indigenous people, grew from around 250 to 1,500, with around 9,500 throughout New Netherland.

On Monday January 21, 1658, a case was presented to the court regarding "Claas Van Elslandt, the Elder, [versus] Raaghel van Thienhoven [defendant plaintiff]" and the age-old problem of mishandled death-care fees. Van Elslandt demanded "payment of Church money for a grave in which the [defendant's] Mother lies, and says that her friends told him, that she had given her husband the money and he had taken it with him in a pocket handkerchief."

If the residents of New Amsterdam's Old Graveyard had received the honor of being reinterred in the new one, then the removal hire didn't do a thorough job of it. In the *Manual of the Corporation of the City of New York for 1856*, one of many illustrated, detailed records of municipal occurrences compiled by Common Council clerk David Thomas Valentine, he details a cellar excavation on Broadway and Morris Street, whereupon workmen discovered "a great many skulls and other relics of humanity." Further on he writes, "It was thought to be proven, that the first comers from Holland established their earliest fortification on this spot, and within its inclosure [*sic*] interred their dead." Meanwhile, the new graveyard, established either in the last years of New Amsterdam or in the first years of British colonial New York, would be incorporated into the Anglican Trinity Churchyard.

Manhattan had a population of approximately five thousand when the construction of Trinity Church on Broadway was completed in 1697. In 1702, the city granted the adjacent and now not-so-new New Graveyard land to Trinity Church to be "appropriated for the public Church yard and burial place of this Citty [*sic*] for ever." It is one of the oldest cemeteries in the five New York City boroughs along with the seventeenth-century (or early eighteenth-century) African Burial Ground, Saint Mark's Church in-the-Bowery and First Shearith Israel Graveyards in Manhattan; Old Gravesend and Flatbush/Flatlands/New Utrecht Dutch Reformed Cemeteries in Brooklyn; and Prospect, Saint George's and Friends Cemeteries in Queens. The oldest-surviving Trinity Churchyard headstone with distinguishable writing predates the first Trinity Church and belongs to five-year-old Richard Churcher, who died in 1681.

Trinity Church was built with the help of the legendary pirate Captain Kidd, who, while on the waiting list for a pew that he would never use because of his ill-timed execution, was generous enough to lend a pulley system to assist with its construction. Piracy, a common keeping-up-with-the-colonies game in the seventeenth and eighteenth centuries, was fully approved of by the English governor of New York, Benjamin Fletcher, who saw to it that the Church of England structure and surrounding land was granted a charter from King William III. A second Trinity Church was

Grave of Alexander Hamilton at Trinity Church.

consecrated in 1790 after the first church perished in the 1776 Great Fire of New York. The third, final and current Gothic Revival Trinity Church, consecrated in 1846 and designed by Richard Upjohn, was the tallest building in the United States until 1869. The cemetery would endure through each new structure.

Many of the residents of Trinity Churchyard are separated by fewer than six degrees as the following list demonstrates: Francis Lewis, a Welsh merchant and the only signee of the Declaration of Independence to be buried in Manhattan; fellow revolutionary Alexander Hamilton, killed in a duel in 1804 in Weehawken by

Vice President Aaron Burr; Hamilton's eldest son, Philip, who was also killed in a Weehawken duel in 1801 by George Eacker, a lawyer and friend of Aaron Burr (Eacker, who died in 1804 from tuberculosis, is interred a few blocks north at Trinity's second cemetery, Saint Paul's Churchyard; his fiancée, Harriet, went on to marry commercial steamboat inventor Robert Fulton, who is buried at Trinity); and British-born Major General Horatio Gates, best known for attempting to take over from General George Washington in the Revolutionary War, for winning the Battle of Saratoga in 1777 and for losing the Battle of Camden in 1780. Gates was also vice president of the New York–founded Society of the Cincinnati, which joined together officers of the Continental army and their descendants. Named after and inspired by the Roman statesman Lucius Quinctius Cincinnatus, who took the reins of power when Rome was under attack and then relinquished his leadership when order was restored, the fraternity's first members included Alexander Hamilton and George Washington. Cincinnati, Ohio, grew from a settlement named after the society.

James Lawrence, who was given posthumous membership to the Society of Cincinnati, is another well-connected resident of Trinity Churchyard. Famous for hollering the demand turned general knowledge quote "Don't give up the ship" during the War of 1812, he did, in fact, make the command, die and lose said ship in 1813. His command nevertheless continues to be a battle cry for the U.S. Navy. Members of his esteemed family of high-ranking political, legal and military figures—the descendants of Sir Robert Lawrence, a twelfth-century knight who fought alongside Richard the Lionheart in the Crusades—are interred in two remaining private family graveyards in Astoria and Bayside in Queens.

The construction of another Trinity Parish church, Saint George's Chapel on Beekman Street to the east, was completed in 1752 for the growing parish. More than a century later, when the congregation moved north and the street grid stretched the existing roads, the Saint George burial vaults were dug up and the inhabitants reinterred at Trinity and elsewhere. If only from city expansion, the New York dead are accustomed to turning in their graves.

Saint Paul's Chapel, completed in 1766, is another extension of Trinity Parish and a little farther north up Broadway. George Washington had his own pew and attended the chapel on his Inauguration Day on April 30, 1789. Having survived the Great Fire of New York in 1776 and the 9/11 terrorist attacks of 2001, after which it became a haven for rescue activity and a shrine to those still missing, Saint Paul's is Manhattan's oldest and only colonial-era church.

In Saint Paul's Churchyard, the Irish are well represented. General Richard Montgomery from Dublin, after whom many cities and counties around the United States are named, was killed early on in the Revolutionary War on New Year's Eve 1775, during the Battle of Quebec. Montgomery was buried the day after his death following an earlier attempt to retrieve his body from the snow by future vice president Aaron Burr. The weight of his death was felt on both sides of the Atlantic. In January 1776, Congress commissioned its first ever monument as a memorial to Montgomery. Its rendering by French sculptor Jean-Jacques Caffieri was supervised by Benjamin Franklin, who by then had become the first American diplomat in France. It was installed at Saint Paul's east window in June 1788 as a symbol of the Patriot cause but had to wait until 1818 to be joined by Montgomery's remains, sent back from Canada and reinterred inside the chapel. Elsewhere at Saint Paul's churchyard, two obelisks honor two United Irishmen, neither one of whom are buried there. One of the honorees is Galway-born William James MacNeven, a physician and chemistry professor who is widely considered to be the "Father of American Chemistry." As a result of marrying into the Riker family, from where Rikers Island gets its name, he is buried in a back garden in Queens belonging to the seventeenth-century Riker-Lent-Smith Homestead. Despite MacNeven being a Catholic, St. Paul's voted to erect a thirty-two-foot cenotaph dedicated to him. Before MacNeven's death, he bankrolled a monument to his friend, Cork-born Thomas Addis Emmet, another United Irishman who was the New York State attorney general and older brother of Robert Emmet, the leader and martyr of the 1803 Irish Rebellion. Thomas Emmet was buried at Saint Mark's Church in-the-Bowery and then reinterred at Glasnevin Cemetery in Dublin in 1922.

Many of the older headstones at the two downtown Trinity churchyards have a familiar antiquated aesthetic: chalky or tawny sandstone tablets, with a rounded head-like top bounded by two upright ears and etched with angels or skull and crossbones. A popular artisanal eighteenth-century line of red and brown sandstone grave markers were meticulously engraved and delivered to the colonies by master craftsman and stonecutter Ebenezer Price from Elizabethtown, New Jersey. Some of his headstones still survive in the older cemeteries of northern New Jersey, where they can be identified by his carved initials. His workshop apprentices continued his style of craft after his death, and the influence of his precise carving of popular winged soul effigies, or death heads, and elegant font can be seen throughout the colonial-era cemeteries of New York, such as the Dutch Reformed churchyards of Staten Island and Brooklyn, Saint Peter's Episcopal Church Graveyard in

Left: Eighteenth-century grave with winged soul effigy at Grace Episcopal Church in Jamaica, Queens.

Below: Blazing Star Cemetery, also known as the Sleight Family Burial Ground, in Staten Island.

the Bronx, Grace Episcopal Church Cemetery in Queens and the covert family burial grounds of the Sleights and Moore-Jacksons in Staten Island and Queens, respectively.

In 1842, under pressure to provide additional burial space, Trinity Church established another cemetery in the bucolic heights of Upper Manhattan. With Manhattan's Grace Church, Saint Patrick's Cathedral and Washington, D.C.'s Smithsonian Castle still ahead of him, the young architect James Renwick Jr. was hired to design the new cemetery on either side of the split of Bloomingdale Road. Trinity purchased farmland from Richard Carman, adjacent to the estate of artist, naturalist and ornithologist John James Audubon, who is buried beneath a bluestone Celtic cross on the east side of the cemetery. Today, Trinity Church Cemetery and Mausoleum's westside community mausoleum makes it a rare active cemetery in Manhattan. When the Commissioners Plan hauled the street grid farther north and Bloomingdale Road was widened into an extension of Broadway, some roadside graves were forever lost. In 1871, the two halves of the cemetery were connected by a Calvert Vaux–designed suspension bridge that could support a hearse and horses. The bridge lasted until the 1911 construction of the eastside Church of the Intercession, now an independent parish since breaking ties with Trinity in 1976. Bertram Goodhue, who completed his apprenticeship with Renwick's architectural firm, designed the church and is interred inside within a Gothic tomb sculpted by Lee Lawrie.

Every Christmas since 1911, a reading of *'Twas the Night before Christmas* (originally *A Visit From St. Nicholas*) by poet and professor Clement Clarke Moore has taken place at the church ahead of a procession to Moore's graveside. His remains were relocated to uptown Trinity from his original interment spot in the vaults of the Church of Saint Luke's in the Field in Greenwich Village, which he helped found, when the parish moved to Harlem. Clement subdivided the land that he inherited from his British grandfather Captain Thomas Clarke—a Manhattan estate named Chelsea after London's Royal Chelsea Hospital for retired veterans—and sold the plots pursuant to the shape of the encroaching grid pattern. Clement's father was Benjamin Moore, the second Episcopal bishop of New York, the rector of Trinity Church (he is buried in its churchyard) and the man who gave communion to Alexander Hamilton at his deathbed.

The former dwelling of uptown Trinity cemetery resident Eliza Bowen Jumel, the Morris-Jumel Mansion, built in 1765, stands a short distance from the cemetery and is the oldest house in Manhattan. Jumel married seventy-seven-year-old Aaron Burr when she was fifty-eight in 1833 and separated from him four months later. Not coincidentally, she selected Alexander Hamilton Jr., whose father's death had occurred courtesy of Burr's dueling bullet, as her divorce lawyer. The divorce was finalized on the day of Burr's death in 1836. Buried elsewhere in the grounds are members of the Astor family, including John Jacob Astor IV, who sank with the *Titanic*, and Alfred D'Orsay Tennyson Dickens, who fell ill and died on a lecture tour during the 1912 centennial celebration of his father, Charles Dickens's birth. Alfred's death was attributed to "acute indigestion."

3

THE CITY'S BUILDING BLOCKS

In eighteenth-century New York, death was easy to come by. The resourceful reaper lurked in unregulated alcoholic tavern concoctions and in the city's obstacle course of horse and carts and unsupervised rampant pigs. In the nineteenth century, New York City visitor Charles Dickens described one of the many rambling Manhattan pigs thus: "He has only one ear; having parted with the other to vagrant-dogs in the course of his city rambles. But he gets on very well without it; and leads a roving, gentlemanly, vagabond kind of life." Other common killers thrived in the customary murders that come with opportunistic and claustrophobic city life, suicides (categorized as a crime of "self-murder" unless declared an act of lunacy), drownings, and any sort of illness that an as yet unenlightened medical profession had scant knowledge of how to cure except for the adverse textbook shrug of mercury and bloodletting. Meanwhile, a procession of colorful diseases—yellow fever, dysentery, malaria, smallpox, typhus, syphilis and tuberculosis—coquettishly boarded ships from Africa, the West Indies and Great Britain and seduced the steering toward New York's busy convivial ports and accommodating human hosts.

Between 1700 and 1800, at the same time as New York City's Lenape population dwindled close to vanishing point, the European and African population—the latter a combination of enslaved and free—increased from five to sixty thousand, with the population almost doubling in the last decade of the eighteenth century. It was in this century that a pastureland for cattle, invariably known as the Commons, the Fields or the Flat, became

A plan of the city of New York, circa 1755. *Public domain*.

the headquarters for the city. Here, death in New York was challenged with respect to how to govern and control it; how to legally inflict it on those deemed unfit to participate within the boundaries of city rules; how to weaken it against the pull of epidemic forces; and how to forestall it through the implementation of legislation, infrastructure, science and sanitation.

The Common Council, which ordered the construction of an almshouse on the Commons in 1736, was eager to fill it with unsparing categories such as "disorderly persons, parents of Bastard Children, Beggars, Servants running away or otherwise misbehaving themselves, Trespassers, Rogues, Vagabonds, poor persons refusing to work, and on their refusal to work and labor, to correct them by moderate whipping, etc," according to the *Minutes of the Common Council of the City of New York, 1675–1776*.

In 1757, a burial ground was fashioned close by. At the same time, the Commons gained two new structures: the Upper Barracks, built in response to the city residents' objection to quartering soldiers during the French and Indian War, and the New Gaol, destined to become the debtors' prison. Previously, criminals had been locked up in the old City Hall on Wall Street where Federal Hall now stands. Bridewell Prison was partially built in 1768, west of the almshouse but not completed until the end of the Revolutionary War. In 1838, it was replaced by an Egyptian Revival–style prison with a new gallows space, the New York City Halls of Justice and House of Detention, better known as "the Tombs." A fourth version of the Tombs, formally named the Manhattan Detention Complex, exists today in Chinatown.

The British used Bridewell and the debtors' prison—renamed the Provost Prison—during the Revolutionary War for Patriot prisoners. Due to the horrific conditions of British imprisonment, more Americans died in jails and prison ships than the total sum of both sides on the battlefields throughout the entire conflict.

Across Centre Street from the old Commons, through the arches and on the rear side of the David N. Dinkins Municipal Building stands a peculiar relic that is so often missed. In 1763, Henry Cuyler built a six-story sugar house that was used as a refinery and warehouse for sugar and molasses on the corner of what is now William (formerly Rose) and Duane Streets. When the Act of Forfeiture was passed after the Revolutionary War, the Loyalist Cuylers were forced to forfeit their right to own property. Cuyler's sugar house was sold at auction to shipping merchant William Rhinelander, after which the building became known as Rhinelander's Sugar House. During the war, the British used the New York sugar houses—including the Van Cortlandt (on the northwest corner of Trinity Church yard) and Livingston (on Crown, now Liberty Street) sugar houses—as prisons for American Patriots. The majority of prisoners, trapped in cramped conditions with meager, maggot-infested rations, died from starvation and disease. The British disposed of the dead with makeshift burials or, in the case of the prison ships, by throwing the bodies overboard.

As to whether or not the Rhinelander Sugar House was a prison, a topic on which doubt has been cast, when it was demolished in 1892, it was decided that two windows were important enough to be saved. One of them was built into the new Rhinelander Building. When that building was razed in 1968 to make way for the NYPD headquarters, the old window and bricks were salvaged once again and put on discreet display behind the David N. Dinkins Municipal Building. Together with the second Rhinelander Sugar House window that was installed in the grounds of the Van Cortlandt Mansion in the Bronx, they are a symbol of freedom from the shackles of colonialism and a gloomy reminder of the cruel circumstances of the American death toll during the Revolutionary War.

For years after the war, at Walloon Bay, just across the East River from Manhattan's Rhinelander Sugar House window, the bones of the prison ship dead regularly washed up on the shore. When Brooklyn Navy Yard took up residency at the bay in the early nineteenth century, workers began to fill multiple containers with the bones that they found. They were buried in a nearby vault, then reinterred in a crypt at Brooklyn's Fort Greene Park beneath a 149-foot granite Doric column, the Prison Ship Martyrs' Monument, designed by Stanford White. Dedicated in 1908, its plaque commemorates the estimated 11,500 prisoners of war who perished aboard the prison ships. Another Stanford White granite column, at Lookout Hill in Prospect Park, pays tribute to the Maryland 400 of the First Maryland Regiment who protected the retreat of the Continental army during the

Left: Rhinelander Sugar House window in Lower Manhattan.

Below: Second Rhinelander Sugar House window at Van Cortlandt House in the Bronx.

Battle of Brooklyn. In doing so, they were depleted by more than 60 percent. The dead were buried by the British in the Gowanus neighborhood in an area that historians and archaeologists are keen to investigate further.

By the end of the war in 1783, the Commons' cemetery was running out of space. Two years later, another cemetery was added at the rear of the old barracks, while a section of the barracks was converted into a hospital extension. Piles of mounting dead were shifted to a pauper's grave—or potter's field—beyond the city limits. Peaking three times in 1795, 1799 and

1803, yellow fever, a viral disease spread by mosquitoes and characterized by jaundice, fever and vomiting blood, brought about the New York City Board of Health in 1805, which morphed into the present-day New York City Department of Health and Mental Hygiene.

In the 1790s, the Common Council leased a mansion, situated a little less than three miles north of the city, for the sick of the almshouse and infirmary to be relocated away from Lower Manhattan. The name of the mansion that the council would later purchase was Bel-Vue (Beautiful View). It had once belonged to Lindley Murray, a Quaker lawyer and writer best known for his English language grammar books used in schools in England and the United States, whose family gave the Murray Hill neighborhood its name. From the mansion came the almshouse, followed by Bellevue Hospital in 1816. In 1866, Bellevue's dead house officially became the City Morgue, and the first civilian hospital photographic department was added soon after. Photographer Oscar G. Mason's portraits of the unclaimed were hung on the Wall of the Unknown Dead for up to a year.

In 1816 and 1817, the vacated Commons' almshouse (built in 1797 to replace the first almshouse) gained surprising new tenants, New York's oldest museum—the New-York Historical Society—and Scudder's American Museum. The latter, which moved into its own building a little to the south and across from Saint Paul's Chapel, was acquired by P.T. Barnum in 1841 and renamed Barnum's American Museum. It burned down in 1865, then resurfaced between Spring and Prince Streets, where it burned down again in 1868. According to fraternal folklore, while the second museum was still standing, a group of gregarious male theater performers visited with the purpose of finding a suitable animal, alive or stuffed, to replace the conspicuous name they already had. Eager to defy the drinking laws that prohibited the sale of alcoholic spirits on Sundays, the Jolly Corks would gather at a boardinghouse on Elm Street. Their antics extended to charity after a member died, and the club endeavored to assist with the burial arrangements of present and future members. As the folklore story continues (one of several), from Barnum's American Museum exhibits, the Jolly Corks chose an elk to represent them, and so the boozy all-male philanthropic Jolly Corks became the Benevolent and Protective Order of Elks. In 1939, Mayor of New York Fiorello La Guardia, himself an Elk, renamed Elm Street "Elk Street" in honor of the fraternal order's first meeting place. Today, the Elks have over 1.5 million members. The monuments and headstones of their burial plots depict the initials of their

Symbol for the Benevolent and Protective Order of Elks at Ocean View Cemetery in Staten Island.

fraternity and an elk inside a clock face at the eleventh hour, representing the late-night meeting of the original postshow theater performers and the hour of their "toast to the absent brothers."

The construction of City Hall, one of the oldest continuously functioning city halls in the United States, took place between 1803 and 1812, and the Commons officially became City Hall Park. Since the 1990s, excavation research has been conducted and overseen by several organizations in advance of a structural upgrade. Among the fragments of ceramics, pipes, kitchenware, building structures, furniture, bottles, glass and animal bones, intact human burials have been discovered as well as a large number of scattered bones. The burial ground, believed to contain the inmates of the Commons institutions, existed in the northern part of City Hall Park in the area of the present-day Tweed Courthouse, where the barracks and the debtors' prison once stood. Bone analysis revealed children and adults of European origin with overall evidence of poor nutrition. Fragmentary remains were returned to the northeast corner of City Hall Park with a commemorative pavestone plaque.

Just north of City Hall on Chambers Street, the Surrogate's Courthouse, built between 1899 and 1907, was originally constructed as a Hall of Records to relieve the original allocated records space inside the former debtors' prison. The Surrogate's Courthouse continues to house the New York City Department of Records while additionally handling all probate and estate proceedings for people who die with or without a will in New York County.

In New York State, if a decedent died with assets valued at less than $50,000, with or without a will, except in some cases of wrongful death or pending lawsuits, then a voluntary administration proceeding, or a small estate, should be filed instead. The legal process that takes place to validate a will is called *probate*. If the decedent has no family or will, then their estate will *escheat*—as in pass—to New York State.

On the cornice of the Surrogate's Courthouse, among the eight sculpted figures of prominent New York leaders, is DeWitt Clinton, nephew of founding father and former vice president George Clinton. DeWitt Clinton was a United States senator, the sixth governor of New York State, the mayor of the city for three terms and the "Father of the Erie Canal," due to his presiding over its construction. When he died from heart failure at the age of fifty-eight in 1828, he was honored with a state funeral. After the grand ceremony, however, his wife and children had nowhere to put him. Clinton's municipal management may have been efficient, but his own financial affairs were appallingly mismanaged. His family were left penniless. Luckily, a friend of Clinton's and a fellow Freemason donated a burial plot at the Little Britain Cemetery in Albany. When Green-Wood Cemetery in Brooklyn began looking for a high-profile resident to attract business, it arranged with Dewitt Clinton's family to have him dug up and put in a temporary Green-Wood vault until he was finally reinterred in 1853 beneath an impressive bronze statue and bas-relief panel depicting the construction of the Erie Canal.

DeWitt's wife and children were not alone in their financial woes. Married women were not allowed to take out insurance in New York State until a law was passed on April 1, 1840. The Presbyterian Synods in Philadelphia and New York founded America's first life insurance company in 1759, called the Corporation for Relief of Poor and Distressed Widows and Children of Presbyterian Ministers. At a later date, the name was mercifully shortened to Presbyterian Ministers Fund. In 1841, Nautilus Mutual Life opened on Wall Street. In 1846, the company began insuring the lives of enslaved persons for slaveholders, even though New York legislature had abolished slavery in 1827. Sales made in the southern states where slavery hadn't yet been abolished made up one-third of Nautilus life insurance policies. As the death claims mounted from hazardous slave labor, the company finally voted against selling policies on enslaved people in 1848. A year later, Nautilus Mutual Life changed its name to the New York Life Insurance Company. In 1894, New York Life became the first American insurance company to offer policies to women and men at an equal price. Upon completion of New York Life's Cass Gilbert–designed neo-Gothic skyscraper on Madison Avenue in 1928, its shining pyramid roof struck gold into the Manhattan skyline.

The Metropolitan Life Insurance Company Tower, another gold-topped skyscraper landmark, stands just two blocks south on Madison Avenue. MetLife began as the National Union Life and Limb Insurance Company for Union soldiers in 1863. On February 15, 1909, a freak accident led to one of Woodlawn Cemetery's strangest epitaphs, which reads like an urgent telegram: "Lost life by stab in falling on ink eraser, evading six young women trying to give him birthday kisses in office Metropolitan Life Building." Office boy George Spencer Millet's fifteenth birthday just happened to fall on the day after Valentine's Day. This may have added to the office ladies' impetus for hunting him down with kisses. While Millet was wriggling away from them, the ink eraser knife in his pocket pierced his heart, planting one final kiss of death.

Propelled by the commissioner's 1811 gridiron street plan (from where the *grid* gets its name), which consisted of 12 north–south avenues and 155 cross streets, yet held back by the wait for a sophisticated underground sewage system (seventy miles of networking sewer pipes would be laid between 1850 and 1855), Manhattan pushed north with all its might through the early nineteenth century, propelled by fear of almost everything at its clogged rear end. The miasma theory of contagion by way of polluted vapor was a common belief that persevered until it was replaced by the germ theory in the latter half of the 1800s.

Grave of George Spencer Millet at Woodlawn Cemetery in the Bronx. *Hermis Pena/ The Woodlawn Cemetery and Conservancy.*

The phrase "Someone is walking over my grave" comes to mind when confronted with the 1809 city ordinance that banned burials beneath streets. In 1823, the Common Council and its Board of Health prohibited burials below Canal Street. In the next decade, another prohibition banned burials below Fourteenth Street. Between 1820 and 1830, the population of Manhattan increased by over 60 percent to more than 202,000. Droves of diseases including the 1832 cholera epidemic that killed around 3,500 people, wreaked havoc on the overcrowded city. Nineteenth-century New York was a dangerous place to be if you were poor, or worse, poor and foreign. The steady stream of immigrant arrivals presented easy targets for shifting blame, lest the entire New York sanitation system and water supply be reconsidered and redeveloped for a costly fee. Dutifully and frequently overcrowded slums emboldened the death toll. The smell alone, from the interminable stacking of dead bodies, provided a solid reason for seeking sanitary alternatives to the routine burial model. It is no wonder that the wealthy sought out graveyard privacy like an after-hours members' club.

The half-acre New York Marble Cemetery, incorporated in 1831, is tucked away inside an East Village block behind an iron-gated alleyway. Although it was the first nonsectarian burial place in Manhattan open to the public, it certainly wasn't egalitarian regarding cost and class. Its two-thousand-plus inhabitants, who came from old and new money, desired a burial space away from the pestilent riffraff. Inspired by the venture, a handful of businessmen built the New York City Marble Cemetery the following year, just one block away. Both cemeteries are made up of vaults.

On June 5, 1823, the *Evening Post* published a letter from physician, botanist and professor Dr. David Hosack (the founder of one of New York's first botanical gardens—Elgin Botanic Garden—where Rockefeller Center now stands, and one of the founders of the New York Historical Society) that expressed his displeasure with aspects of the 1823 burial ban below Canal Street. "The burial in graves, where the earth is frequently disturbed, and where the bodies cannot be placed at a sufficient depth below the surface, is certainly liable to some of the objections that have been urged; but the interment in vaults is well known to be free from the evils referred to." When Hosack, whose medical services were summoned to the bedsides of two dying duelists, Philip Hamilton and three years later his father, Alexander Hamilton, died in 1835, he was interred inside a vault at the New York Marble Cemetery. Over fifty years later, his descendants had him relocated to Trinity Churchyard.

The marble that gives both the New York and New York City Marble Cemeteries their names is of the Tuckahoe variety, and it is found in southern New York State and neighboring Connecticut. Marble was believed to be a superior class of disease-resistant material compared with common soil. Furthermore, the attractive white Tuckahoe marble has been used to bedeck the city with landmark structures such as Saint Patrick's Cathedral and the Washington Square Arch. It is not accidental that the government of New York State chose the village of Ossining in Westchester County, local to Tuckahoe quarries, as the site of a new state prison, Sing Sing, in 1825.

Though they are connected by familial ties, almost identical names and metamorphic rock, New York Marble Cemetery and New York City Marble Cemetery have always been separate entities. In both cemeteries, descendants who can prove their lineage are allowed to be buried within the available spaces in the vaults of their ancestors. At the time of writing, New York Marble Cemetery has a couple of vaults available for purchase at the cost of a few grand, a steal for the vicinity of Manhattan.

In the rectangular lawn-shaped New York Marble Cemetery, once billed as "the resting place of gentlemen," the 156 marble vaults, built in pairs without a connecting passageway, are positioned ten feet underground and can be accessed by digging into the lawn, removing the stone slabs fixed into the ground and climbing down a ladder. There are no markers; instead, marble plaques are attached to the cemetery walls. Notable burials include chief engineer of the Erie Canal Benjamin Wright; tobacco tycoon Peter Lorillard II; prominent New York Dutch families such as the Beeckmans, Hones, Hoyts, Varicks, Van Zandts and Quackenbushes; and the Huguenot DuBois clan, whose descendant Caroline Dubois is one of the cemetery trustees.

Unlike the New York Marble Cemetery, the New York City Marble Cemetery is visible from the street through its wrought-iron fence and gate. Its 258 underground vaults have markers laid out on the ground that can be lifted open to provide entry. Residents include James Lenox, co-founder of the New York Public Library and the founder of Presbyterian Hospital; a number of New York mayors; several members of the Roosevelt family; the Kip family, after whom the Kips Bay neighborhood in the East Midtown area is named; and explorer and writer John Lloyd Stephens, who is credited with rediscovering the Mayan civilization and planning the Panama Railroad. Founding father and fifth president James Monroe, the third president to have died on Independence Day—on the fifty-fifth anniversary of the Declaration of Independence—five years to the day after the joint deaths of fellow presidents John Adams and Thomas Jefferson, was interred in 1831 in his son-in-law's vault. In 1858, Monroe was reclaimed by his native Virginia and reinterred in Richmond. Among the more unusual names at the New York City Marble Cemetery are Mangle Minthorne Quackenbos and Preserved Fish. To add to the oddities, in 2010, a caretaker found military-grade plastic explosives buried near the rear of the cemetery, luckily without a detonator. Who put it there and for what reason remains one of New York's many mysteries.

4
BODY SNATCHING AND OTHER MISDEMEANORS

In *A Journal of the Plague Year*, published in 1772, *Robinson Crusoe* author Daniel Defoe writes of the new rule put forth by the mayor of London amid England's bubonic plague of 1665 that graves should be "at least six feet deep." If this was in fact the origin of the "six feet under" idiom, then the colonies paid little heed. The advancement of medical science in the Age of Enlightenment was such that there was a frantic demand for cadavers to further schooling on anatomy. Henceforth, a niche criminal was born, the *resurrectionist*. Grave robbing, or body snatching, was a popular means to a medical education in Britain and America. In New York, the resurrection men were aided by lazy, shallow graves, sometimes no more than six inches deep.

At present, the City of New York requirements are as follows: "When human remains are buried in the ground, the top of the coffin or casket shall be at least three feet below the level of the ground, but if the coffin or casket is enclosed in a concrete or metal vault, the top of the vault shall be at least two feet below the level of the ground."

In 1771, King George III granted a royal charter to establish New York Hospital for "medical treatment, chirurgical management and maniacs." Construction began in 1773, but the hospital's completion was delayed by two successive inconveniences: a fire and a revolution. During the Revolutionary War, British and Hessian soldiers used the remaining structure as a barracks. In the early years of American Independence and a few years before the building officially opened as the New York Hospital in 1791, a small section of it was occupied by an anatomy class taught by Dr. Richard Bayley, a noted physician who had himself studied in London with the Scottish surgeon William Hunter, after whom Glasgow's anatomical specimen Hunterian Museum is named. (London's Hunterian Museum is named after John Hunter, William's younger brother.)

Public outrage at grave robbing incidents was significantly heightened when the resurrectionists switched from the Negro's Burying Ground to Trinity Churchyard. In February 1788, the *New York Daily Advertiser* published a letter from someone called "Humanio," who set down the graphic indignities carried out by the resurrectionists:

> *Human flesh has been taken up along the docks, sewed up in bags; and that this horrid practice is pursued to make a merchandize of human bones, more than for the purpose of improvement in Anatomy.…If a law was passed, prohibiting the bodies of any other than Criminals from being dissected, unless by particular desire of the dying…for the benefit of mankind, a stop might be put to the horrid practice here; and the minds of a very great number of my fellow-liberated, or still enslaved Blacks, quieted. By publishing this, you will greatly oblige both them, and your very humble servant.*

New York medical students plundered cemeteries because no cadaver-providing service existed. Unlike Europe, for the larger part of the eighteenth century in America, the remains of executed criminals were not donated to the advancement of medical science, and the dissection of the human form was commonly viewed as both impious and repellent. In April 1788, a medical student gamely dangled—or waved—an arm that wasn't his out of the window of the makeshift anatomy school at the New York Hospital in front of a group of boys outside. When one of the

New York Hospital on 1852 map. *Public domain.*

boys advanced toward the window to take a closer look, the student told him that the dismembered arm belonged to the boy's mother. Whether the medical student was being flippant or had knowledge that the boy's mother had recently died is unclear. As the popular version of the story continues, the boy's father, upon being told of this encounter, promptly dug up his wife's grave for confirmation and found only her absence. It is not difficult to see how public unrest might ensue from these events. Brewing outrage was already in place due to local press reports of the resurrectionists' careless body snatching. Soon enough, a mob gathered outside Bayley's laboratory, and the 1788 Doctors' Riot began.

According to a letter addressed to the governor of Virginia from Virginia planter, former Revolutionary colonel and state commissioner William Heth, who, as fate would have it, was visiting New York on matters of state diplomacy, the crowd broke into the anatomy laboratory, where they found "three fresh bodies—one, boiling in a kettle, and two others cutting up—with certain parts of the two sex's hanging up in a most brutal position."

In response to the mob's ransacking, the mayor of New York, James Duane, after whom Duane Street, which runs south of the former New York Hospital site, is named (keeping with the medical theme, Duane Street, along with Reade Street one block south, provided the name for the New York pharmacy chain Duane Reade, the first of which was situated between the two streets on Broadway), sent the students to jail as a temporary safehouse. The riot lasted a few days, during which medical professionals around the city were hunted down. Alexander Hamilton's attempts to prevent the raiding of his former school, Columbia College (later Columbia University), whose medical department was the first in America to grant the Doctor of Medicine degree, failed miserably. An estimated half a dozen to twenty people were killed in the riot. In the aftermath, armed guards stood watch over the cemeteries.

In 1789, in response to the riot, New York passed legislation that allowed executed criminals to be dissected. Then in 1790, the Crimes Act, a "comprehensive statute defining an impressive variety of federal crimes" authorized that "the court before whom any person shall be convicted of the crime of murder, for which he or she shall be sentenced to suffer death, may at their discretion, add to the judgment, that the body of such offender shall be delivered to a surgeon for dissection." New York University School of Medicine cofounder John William Draper from St. Helens, England, was the first to propose "An Act to Promote Medical Science and Protect Burial Grounds." The Bone Bill passed in 1854 by one vote. Draper's conditions, that "all vagrants dying, unclaimed, and without friends, are to be given to institutions in which medicine and surgery are taught for dissection" must have registered as a lifestyle revision for solitary drifters. Family members were allowed up to twenty-four hours to claim their relative for burial before the deceased was offered up for dissection.

In 1878, at Saint Mark's Church in-the-Bowery, grave robbers stole the remains of Irish-born dry goods millionaire Alexander Turney Stewart.

While there is no evidence that his body was recovered, there is a persistent legend in which Stewart's wife paid the ransom even though she was never quite sure if the remains were his, and as a safety measure, fitted his reinterment mausoleum in Long Island with a security device linked to the bells of a cathedral.

During the last quarter of the twentieth century, a funeral parlor in East Harlem owned by Timothy O'Brien accommodated the mixed ethnicities of New York, including Muslim immigrants, some of whom crossed state lines during a time when few funeral homes catered to a range of faiths. Islamic custom requires a swift burial after the body is washed, scented and wrapped in a shroud with the head pointed toward Mecca. O'Brien also welcomed and embalmed those who had died from AIDS-related illnesses during the 1980s and early 1990s at a time when many fearful New York funeral homes refused to do so. His pioneering funeral business received column inches for its generosity and tolerance. Then in 2006, Timothy O'Brien reappeared in the press for a very different reason.

That same year, the Food and Drug Administration shut down Biomedical Tissue Services in Fort Lee, New Jersey, after the company's owner Dr. Michael Mastromarino and members of his staff were charged with stealing human body tissue and bones. An NYPD investigation found that Mastromarino had made a deal with a number of undertakers, including O'Brien, whom he paid around $1,000 per corpse. The bones that were extracted by Mastromarino and his team from selected bodies awaiting burial or cremation were replaced with plastic piping. The Biomedical Tissue Services scandal became international news in 2005 after it was revealed that the remains of the deceased writer and broadcaster Alistair Cooke, famous for *Letter from America* and *Masterpiece Theater*, were among those that had been violated. Cooke died from lung cancer that had spread to his bones. An assemblage of those bones, stolen from O'Brien's New York Mortuary Service Inc., were sold for $7,000 in 2004 and accompanied by an altered death certificate that omitted Cooke's cause of death and reduced his age from ninety-five to eighty-five. In 2006, seven funeral directors, including O'Brien and others from the Bronx and Brooklyn, pleaded guilty to their individual body theft collusion charges. In 2008, Mastromarino was sentenced by the Brooklyn Supreme Court to serve eighteen to fifty-four years. He died five years later, at the age of forty-nine, from liver cancer that had spread to his bones.

In 2000, when checking on her dead relatives at a Cypress Hills Cemetery mausoleum on the Queens/Brooklyn border, Florida resident Barbara Davis

Alistair Cooke. *Public domain.*

got more and indeed less than she probably expected. One of her aunts was missing, while another aunt, though present, was missing her head. A spate of bodysnatching break-ins had taken place during the previous decade. In 1991, twenty-one-year-old Matias Frias stole five skulls from three Cypress Hills mausoleums. Skulls can sell for thousands, and in Frias's case, his buyers desired them as the essential props for the spirit tampering rituals of Palo Mayombe, an Afro-Caribbean religion that originated in the Congo and then traveled via the slave trade to Cuba and beyond.

Grave robbery still goes on in North America, but most often it is committed by fortune seekers looking for valuables that are either buried with the bodies or in the decorative memorial items around the grave. When Queens local Anthony Casamassima came into the possession of a passkey due to working as a caretaker for Saint John Cemetery (until he was fired for stealing a pedestal), he used it to break into multiple mausoleums in the New York Metropolitan Area, including the Cemetery Belt's Cypress Hills, Salem Fields and All Faiths Cemeteries. Over a period of two decades, in the dead of night, Casamassima stole valuable funerary art including priceless urns and Tiffany stained-glass windows. For the Tiffany theft, he used the *Tiffany Windows* book by all-round antiques expert, FBI art theft investigation advisor and former senior vice president of Christie's Auction House Alastair Duncan as his guide. In a bizarre twist of fate, Duncan became an accomplice to Casamassima's nocturnal activities.

Several years after stealing a nine-foot Tiffany window from a mausoleum in Brooklyn's Salem Fields Cemetery, Casamassima offered to sell it to Bronx antique dealer Lawrence Zinzi, who then put him in touch with Duncan. Zinzi and Duncan subsequently purchased the window for $60,000 and then sold it for $219,980 to Japanese collector Takeo Horiuchi for his Tiffany museum in Nagoya, Japan. Amid the FBI investigation that followed, Casamassima and Zinzi secretly recorded their conversations with Duncan and then testified against him as part of a plea bargain. In March 2000, Duncan was sentenced to two years and three months in a federal prison.

Besides the theft of bodies and funerary art, the death-care industry provides rich pickings for criminal minds. On August 5, 2016, the *Tri-*

County Independent, a Pennsylvania newspaper, published a piece on retired NYPD officer Daniel Austin Sr. who, proudly posing with a framed letter of commendation from an NYPD assistant police chief, was interviewed about his role in Operation Omega, the New York City task force that eventually tracked down "Son of Sam" serial killer David Berkowitz in August 1977. In a similar vein to Timothy O'Brien, Austin Sr., in the cemetery business since hanging up his police uniform, would make another, albeit bigger splash in the press for reasons that were far from heroic.

In September 2019, New York State attorney general Letitia James filed a lawsuit against Austin Sr. for mismanagement of All Faiths Cemetery in Queens. Founded by the Prussian Lutheran pastor Reverend Frederick William Geissenhainer, the nonsectarian All Faiths Cemetery, formerly the Lutheran Cemetery, has over half a million interments. Its website emphasizes its "user friendly Filming Location with the Mayor's Office of Film Production" alongside a list of TV and film credits that includes *Rosemary's Baby*. All Faiths is noteworthy for its memorial monument dedicated to the 1,021-person death toll from the PS *General Slocum* pleasure boat disaster after it caught fire on the East River in 1904, and for the Trump plot, where former president Donald Trump's parents, grandparents and older brother are interred.

The Trump plot at All Faiths Cemetery in Middle Village, Queens.

A routine audit of assets by the New York State Division of Cemeteries found that Daniel Austin Sr., the former president and chairman of the not-for-profit state-regulated cemetery, and "Son of Austin," Daniel Austin Jr., who took over as president upon his father's retirement, had allegedly dipped into the cemetery's charitable assets for their own gain, enabling Austin Sr. to give himself a $900,000 retirement award in 2014, despite continuing on as chairman. Austin Jr., also an ex-cop, was accused of embezzling $63,000 in unchecked bonuses. Other All Faiths board members were implicated in using restricted cemetery assets to provide mortgage loans to family members.

In 2007, Anthony Sparno, an Italian American originally from the Belmont area of the Bronx, gave an interview to the *New York Times* in which his conversion to Islam was referenced in relation to his job at the Jersey State Memorial Park, otherwise known as Makbarat As-Salaam, in Millstone, New Jersey. New York City's Muslim population has no exclusive burial ground within the five boroughs and often uses Islamic cemeteries in Long Island and New Jersey. In 2017, Sparno, who was the president of the Jersey State Memorial Park Board of Trustees from 2005 until 2011, and the previous president, Joseph Carlino, were accused of defrauding the cemetery and embezzling hundreds of thousands of dollars from the illegal sales of thousands of graves.

In April 2013, Arthur Friedman, president of the United Hebrew Cemetery in Richmond, Staten Island, and his wife, Ilana, the cemetery administrator, were convicted of grand larceny charges. Ilana, who had stolen approximately $1 million between 2005 and 2011 to pay for shopping sprees and vacations, was sentenced to five years' probation. She and her husband were henceforth banned from working in the funeral industry. In February 2014, Timothy Griffin, a real estate lawyer and the acting UHB president who replaced the disgraced Friedmans, was arrested for embezzling nearly $2 million from the same cemetery fund in order to replace the money that he'd stolen from his law practice clients and also to purchase a BMW and country club membership. Less fortunate than the Friedmans, Griffin received a prison sentence.

In the nineteenth century, the notorious Five Points neighborhood of Lower Manhattan was in perpetual need of funeral services. In 1888, when Italian immigrants had a firm hold on the restructured slums, Charles (Carlo) Bacigalupo, a celebrated local figure who had emigrated from Genoa in his boyhood, founded the first of his Little Italy funeral homes. Over the last few decades, much of what used to constitute Little Italy has been swallowed up by the surrounding neighborhoods of SoHo, Chinatown and Nolita, and businesses like Bacigalupo's have changed hands accordingly. The southern end of Mulberry Street, where one of Bacigalupo's old funeral homes still has his name carved above the entrance, is colloquially known as "Funeral Row" due to its compact chain of Chinese funeral homes, supplies and florists.

Many of Chinatown's dead are interred at Cypress Hills Cemetery, where tiny, weathered headstones mark the graves of the first wave of Chinese migration to New York, and where the Qingming Festival, at which the graves of Chinese ancestors are cleaned and adorned with ritual offerings, takes place annually. Slain members of the organized Chinatown crime gangs—the Hip Sing Tong and the On Leong Tong—who battled one another during the early twentieth century, and whose funerals were often arranged by Bacigalupo's funeral parlor, sometimes with an Italian marching

Old Chinese plot at Cypress Hills Cemetery in Cypress Hills, Brooklyn.

band, were buried at Cypress Hills and later repatriated in China for their "second burial" in ancestral graves, a popular custom prior to the Chinese Communist Revolution.

When the Godfather of Chinatown, Benny Ong of the Hip Sing Tong, died in 1994, his funeral was organized by the Wah Wing Sang Funeral Corporation, which owns the old Bacigalupo parlor. Twenty years later, Wah Wing Sang accidentally cremated a Buddhist woman against her family's wishes, who then filed a lawsuit against the funeral home at the Brooklyn Supreme Court. A less devastating mix-up occurred in 2011 when a staff member of the Fook On Sing Funeral Supplies store, also on Funeral Row, was arrested for selling counterfeit goods. The store owners explained that they were actually cardboard and paper copies of luxury goods, designed as symbolic gifts to be burned at Chinese funerals.

From the 1950s and for more than half a century, the M. Marshall Blake Funeral Home, owned by Marguerite Marshall, née Blake, at St. Nicholas Place in the Sugar Hill section of Harlem, operated out of the James Bailey House—a Châteauesque and Romanesque Revival mansion built for former Barnum & Bailey Circus impresario James Bailey in the 1880s. In 2014, a former contestant on the TV show *Storage Wars* discovered dozens of urns and containers in his newly attained Harlem storage unit, full of cremated human remains. An investigation revealed that they had been left there by Marguerite's deceased husband, Warren Blake, a former NYPD detective and the unit's former owner, due to unclaimed remains having been sent back to the funeral organizers from crematoriums.

Accidents and oversights will happen in any line of business. Likewise, misconduct is also a casual residence of work, play and education. The American Academy McAllister Institute in Hell's Kitchen, founded by Dr. John McAllister in 1926 as the McAllister School of Embalming, is New York City's only—and therefore oldest—school for morticians. Dubbed the "Harvard of mortuary schools," AAMI took an ungainly stumble in 2018 when the New York Health Department accused seven teachers, including the AAMI president, of revealing examination answers to their students. Consequently, almost one hundred New York morticians were notified by the New York State Bureau of Funeral Directing that they would lose their licenses if they didn't retake and pass the exam.

The death-care industry presents a unique set of potential problems when it comes to entrusting it. The dead can't complain. Meanwhile, friends and family of the deceased generally aren't privy to bookkeeping misconduct. Fortunately, in other matters of death, the rules regarding the New York cadaver supply for medical and mortuary training recently underwent a momentous, pivotal shift. In May 2016, a *New York Times* investigative piece drew attention to the fact that families were given just forty-eight hours to collect a relative's unclaimed body before the city offered it to medical and mortuary schools. A bill, signed into law by former New York governor Andrew Cuomo in August 2016, banned the use of unclaimed bodies for dissection or embalming practice without written consent by a spouse or next of kin or unless the deceased is a registered body donor.

On March 1, 2017, the New York State Senate passed Senator David Carlucci's bill to make "Lauren's Law" permanent. Named after twelve-year-old heart transplant recipient Lauren Shields, Lauren's Law requires driver's license or state ID applicants to complete the organ donor section instead of having the option to leave it blank. On October 16, 2017, Governor Cuomo signed an executive order directing the Department of Heath to work with the relevant organ and transplant agencies in the state and to develop ways to increase the number of registered organ donors. In New York State, between nine and ten thousand people are currently awaiting an organ transplant. Only 41 percent of state residents are registered organ donors, compared to the 60 percent national average.

5
WE'VE BEEN BURYING IN IT A LONG TIME

In February 1788, a petition signed by New York City's free and enslaved Black residents was submitted to the Common Council regarding the "young gentlemen in this city who call themselves students of the physic," and who "under cover of the night, in the most wanton sallies of excess…dig up bodies of our deceased friends and relatives of your petitioners, carrying them away without respect for age or sex." The piteous condition of the petitioners' plight is highlighted by the fact that they didn't demand that the practice should stop, but instead that the grave robbery be "conducted with the decency and propriety which the solemnity of such occasion requires."

The same burial ground that the petitioners had tried to protect from student surgeon resurrectionists was dug up again two centuries later, and contrary to popular belief, its discovery was not accidental. In December 1990, the General Services Administration (GSA) purchased a plot at 290 Broadway for the construction of the thirty-four-story Ted Weiss Federal Building, named after a Democratic senator. The main tenants of the building have included the Internal Revenue Service, the Environmental Protection Agency and the Federal Bureau of Investigation. The GSA is an independent agency of the U.S. government that was established in 1949 to help manage and provide supplies for federal agencies and employees. In short, the GSA hands the keys over to federal properties.

In 1988, the House of Representatives received a prospectus from the GSA regarding the intended purchase of land for a new office building.

 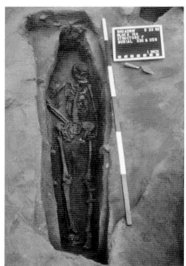

Left: "Negros Burial Ground" on 1754 map. *Public domain.*

Right: Excavation of African Burial Ground. *Public domain.*

Within a year, through an environmental impact statement and analysis of historical maps and colonial documents referring to a "Negro's Burying Ground," the GSA became aware of its potential existence, which meant complying with the National Historic Preservation Act of 1966 as well as the Advisory Council on Historic Preservation. On May 20, 1991, excavators located the first skeleton and quickly discovered that it was not alone. A wider excavation followed in a selected segment of the 6.6-acre burial ground. This chain of events grabbed the attention of the city and anchored its focus directly on its deeply buried history. When New Yorkers were informed of the Manhattan discovery, major concern was expressed regarding the GSA's overall conduct and the handling of the remains at Lehman College. Activists demanded respectful treatment for the site and for the dead. Assorted organizations, concerned citizens, politicians and Harlem's Schomburg Center got involved, and on April 23, 1992, a civic meeting took place at Trinity Church. Mayor David Dinkins established an advisory committee while huge protests led to the suspension and eventual reduction of the Ted Weiss Federal Building plans.

An estimated 15,000 people were interred at the burial ground, which appears on maps in the early 1700s but may have been in use as early as the 1630s. The remains of the 419 people who were disinterred, nearly half of whom were children, were transferred to the Cobb Laboratory of Howard University, a historically Black research-oriented university in Washington, D.C. Anthropologist Dr. Michael Blakey, the director of the African Burial Ground Project, presided over the analysis of the skeletons, artifacts and deposits and, with his team, grappled with the GSA over receiving the necessary research provisions for the better part of a decade.

The weight of two centuries, including the remnants of an eighteenth-century pottery and tannery that had coexisted with the cemetery when it was active and a brick drain that had forced through and beyond an otherwise intact human skeleton, had very nearly pushed the burial ground out of history. The majority of excavated skeletons were found in coffins, some shared by infants and adults. The occasional empty coffins that were discovered support the accusation of grave robbery in the 1788 petition to the Common Council.

Bone analysis revealed evidence of short lives, disease and fractures from strenuous labor. Occasional sets of teeth were filed into points or an hourglass shape. Objects buried with the deceased included coins placed in the hands or on the eyes, jewelry, buttons, toys, pipes and ceramics. A heart-shaped symbol found on a coffin lid was believed to be a *sankofa* (disputed by historian Erik R. Seeman in a 2010 peer review), a symbol traditionally used by the Akan people of Ghana and the Ivory Coast that means "looking back to go forward." Sankofa Park Playground in Brooklyn's East New York neighborhood was renamed after the same symbol. It sits within African Burial Ground Square, where a burial ground existed as far back as the seventeenth century for those enslaved by the local Dutch elite families. Those families—the Schencks (after whom the playground was first named), Duryeas and Rapeljes—who were once buried close by, were relocated by their descendants to the current New Lots Cemetery, which lies adjacent to the square and is adjoined to the Reformed Church, now the New Lots Community Church. In September 1886, an elderly farmer, Stephen Vanderveer, gave his New Lots recollections to the *Brooklyn Daily Eagle*:

> *You may doubt me, but that old graveyard is nearly two hundred years old and many of my ancestors are resting therein; the last one I remember of was my great uncle, Johannes Vanderveer, who died at the ripe old age of 87 years. In those days there were as many negroes as whites in this neighborhood. The latter were buried in front by the roadside and the former away back near the swamp.*

Brooklyn's African Burial Ground continued to be used by African Americans throughout the nineteenth century and is now recognized as such following a historical and archaeological data investigation.

The 419 individual human remains taken from Manhattan's African Burial Ground were returned on October 3, 2003, in mahogany coffins carved in Ghana, and carried by horse-drawn hearses in the last stage of the ceremony called the Rites of Ancestral Return. Wood samples from the original coffins, which had been stored in a freezer at the World Trade Center laboratory, were destroyed two years earlier in the 9/11 terrorist attacks. The route of the procession took in Broadway's ticker tape terrain along the Canyon of Heroes as well as the former domain of the old slave market by Wall Street. The remains were reinterred with traditional African burial rites beneath seven grassy mounds designed to protrude above the lay of the land. In 1993, the African Burial Ground was placed on the National Register of Historic Places and declared a national monument in 2006.

Juan Rodriguez, a free Dominican born to a Portuguese father and an African mother, ticked a remarkable number of New York firsts. He was delivered to Manhattan Island in 1613 by a Dutch sea captain to help set up a trading post and network with the Lenape. Rodriguez stayed behind, learned the local language and may have married a Lenape woman. As such, he was the first nonindigenous resident, the first Black resident and the first Latino resident of New York City. In 2012, a section of Broadway

The Sankofa symbol on the Ancestral Chamber at the African Burial Ground National Monument.

stretching through Little Dominican Republic from Washington Heights into Inwood was named after him.

Thirteen years after the arrival of Rodriguez, in 1626, eleven slaves arrived on the shores of the brand-new colony of New Amsterdam via the Dutch West India Company. Director Willem Kieft turned their 1644 petition for the freedom they expected after almost twenty years in bondage to his advantage. Kieft's War (1643–45), as the name of the conflict suggests, was Kieft's fault. Granting the slaves half freedom (there were many conditions, including the enslavement of any offspring) beyond the fort supplied the colony with a thin layer of protection or borrowed time in the event of an attack from any of the indigenous tribes. The Land of the Blacks, as the area was colloquially known, stretched in patches across the width of Manhattan Island from Fresh Water Pond (also known as Collect Pond) to the Little Africa area of Black-owned farmland in today's Greenwich Village.

The "Negro's Burial Ground" existed outside of the city in a fairly isolated area close to swampland. Many of those buried had been brought to New York from wide geographical distances on the African continent via the West African slave coast, the Caribbean and South America. They adhered to a mix of religions—Christianity, Islam, polytheism and animism. A state law passed in 1702 prohibited the attendance of more than three slaves at a funeral unless they were working on the orders of their master or mistress. During British colonial rule, new laws appeared in quick succession designed to prevent white slave owners from killing their "property" and burying them in secret and Black people from gathering or passing unseen to any opportunistic moment in which nighttime plotting or insurrection could occur. Colonial white fear was stoked by the New York Slave Revolt of 1712 and the Slave Insurrection of 1741, both of which resulted in an excess of grisly executions.

In the early years of the African Burial Ground and in keeping with West African traditions, burials took place at night. In 1722, the Common Council, made up of familiar names from the city's enduring Dutch elite—Roosevelt, Kip, Van Cortlandt and Schuyler—passed a "Law for Regulating the Burial of Slaves" requiring "that all Negroes and Indian Slaves that shall Dye within this Corporation on the South side of the Fresh Water be buryed by day light at or before Sunsett [*sic*]." The "Indian Slaves" were often captured in colonial conflict or simply imported to New York as sale items from as far as the West Indies. The cemetery was closed by the city in 1794, and soon after, the land was scooped up by Manhattan's wealthy, divided into plots and surrendered to the will of real estate for the next two centuries.

At the beginning of the eighteenth century, more than 40 percent of households in New York City, the biggest slave city in the North and second only in the Thirteen Colonies to Charleston, South Carolina, kept slaves. Trinity Church periodically banned or restricted mixed burials in its cemetery and had designated areas for Black communicants, including a "burial ground for negroes" at Church and Reade Streets off Broadway. The Black population of Manhattan increased to approximately ten thousand during the Revolutionary War due to British admiral General Howe's promise of freedom to those who were willing to defend colonial rule. Contrary to the demands of the victorious Patriots, in 1783, the British saw to it that around three thousand Black Loyalists were given safe passage to Nova Scotia. Free Black people were in the minority until after the Revolution, at which point approximately 20 percent of New York City's white households kept at least one slave.

A cautious New York State Gradual Emancipation Law in 1799 granted freedom to enslaved people born after July 4 of that year, but they were required to remain as indentured servants until men and women reached twenty-eight and twenty-five, respectively. An 1817 law liberated slaves born after this date, but it wasn't to be enacted for another ten years. The date of July 4, 1827, did not represent full emancipation either, as children born to slave mothers prior to that date were to remain as indentured servants until they reached twenty-one. All forms of slavery, including bringing in slaves from slave states, were outlawed in 1841. A man named Caesar who served multiple generations of the same family for a whole century in Albany County is believed to be the last manumitted slave—possibly in 1841—in

Caesar, who is believed to be the last enslaved person freed in the state of New York in 1841. *Public domain.*

New York State. His is also one of the few names put forward as the oldest person ever photographed. According to his burial marker, Caesar was born in 1737 and died in 1852, making him 114 or 115 years old at the time of his death. The Atlantic slave trade continued despite the Act to Prohibit the Importation of Slaves in 1807. Illegal slave ships were no stranger to the ports of New York City as a point of departure. Meanwhile, the State of New York continued to profit from southern slave labor and plantation imports until the end of the Civil War in 1865.

After slavery was abolished nationally in that year, the Bethune family in Georgia decided to keep their former slave, a blind teenager called Thomas Greene Wiggins. The genius of Wiggins, aka "Blind Tom," became apparent soon after he and his relatives were sold to the Bethune's Georgia plantation in 1850. Exhibiting behavior consistent with autism, Wiggins was a musical savant. By the age of ten, his precise mimicry, impressive piano playing and composition skills led him to become the first African American to perform at the White House for President James Buchanan. Custody of Wiggins switched to the ex-spouse of one of the Bethune family as he continued to play popular concerts. He moved with his legal guardian to New York City and later Hoboken in New Jersey. Every so often, during his later years, it would be reported somewhere that Blind Tom had died. One such time occurred in 1889, when he was presumed to have been swept away by the Johnstown Flood in Pennsylvania. In 1903, one dubious witness wrote to the *Brooklyn Daily Eagle* claiming to have identified Wiggins's body and his resultant Johnstown tombstone. Blind Tom's most plausible death, however, happened in Hoboken when he was fifty-nine in June 1908.

Despite the headstone at Brooklyn's Evergreens Cemetery with Wiggins's name, face and list of achievements spread out on both sides of it, his presence beneath the soil is elusive. The day after printing Wiggins's obituary, the *New York Times* reported a disagreement among the mourners at the Frank E. Campbell Undertaking Company, a couple of whom claimed that the body in the coffin was not Blind Tom. In 1949, an affidavit surfaced in Georgia, detailing plans by one of the Bethune family to move Blind Tom from a grave near Columbus, Georgia, to the Bethune family plot at another cemetery not far away. The Bethune family member died before the transfer could occur, but how Tom's remains are presumed to have traveled to Georgia in the first place have never been properly explained. His Georgia graveside was even visited and serenaded by jazz trumpeter Dizzy Gillespie in 1979. The two-grave mystery and who lies where may never be solved, but the Evergreens Cemetery records confirm that Wiggins was never disinterred.

Persistent community efforts are the reason why long-forgotten African and African American burial grounds have emerged in recent years, ranging from the study of maps and census records to radar tests and excavations. The list includes the aforementioned Sankofa Park African Burial Ground in Brooklyn, the Enslaved African Burial Ground in Joseph Rodman Drake Park at Hunts Point in the Bronx (the same park contains the fenced-off cemetery headstones of the slave-keeping families, the Willets, Leggetts and Hunts), the cemetery remains of the Low Dutch Church of Harlem (later the Elmendorf Reformed Church) under the defunct 126th Street Bus Depot

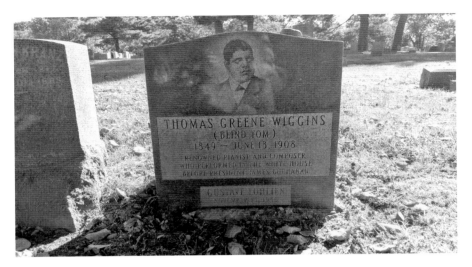

"Blind Tom" at the Evergreens Cemetery in Brooklyn.

in East Harlem and the Saint Philip's Episcopal Church Cemetery on the Lower East Side that is namechecked on a sign at the nearby community garden—M'finda Kalunga Garden—at Sara Roosevelt Park. When the downtown African Burial Ground was closed by the city in 1794, the African Society petitioned the Common Council for a new burial space. Land was granted in the present-day Chrystie Street area the following year. In 1827, the cemetery became the property of the city's first African American Episcopal church—Saint Philip's Church in Centre Street. It remained at the site until 1853, after which the northward push of the city necessitated the transferal of the burials to the mothership of reinterment that is Cypress Hills Cemetery. A 2003 documentary study of the Saint Philip's Episcopal Church Cemetery, prepared by Historical Perspectives Inc. in response to plans for the Second Avenue subway extension, recommended that the potentially burial-sensitive area beneath Chrystie Street be avoided. The report concluded that the area would not be disrupted by the route of the extension. In 2006, nearby excavation work by the New Museum uncovered bone fragments in the wall of an adjacent lot, which were then reinterred at Cypress Hills Cemetery.

As Randall Comfort's *History of Bronx Borough, City of New York*, published in 1906, plainly put it in a section describing the burial grounds around Van Cortlandt House: "It is said that negroes were always interred in 'the back yard of a cemetery.'" Van Cortlandt Park in the Bronx, formerly the Van

Vault Hill at the Van Cortlandt family burial ground in the Bronx.

Cortlandt estate, named after a Dutch mercantile and political family, is now the third-largest park in the city. Van Cortlandt House, constructed by slaves, was the first historic house to open as a museum in New York City in 1897. The Van Cortlandt Family Burial Ground, protected by a high stone wall and iron gate at Vault Hill, lies within walking distance. The fallen headstones of some of the other prominent families in the area have been gathered up from the extinct Kingsbridge burial ground and stacked in a corner next to the Van Cortlandt House. The probable slave burial ground, detected by Department of Agriculture soil and radar tests in 2019, is in an as yet unmarked half acre area close to a path by the lake that the slaves built.

The residents of Upper Manhattan's Nagel Cemetery, in use from the seventeenth century and the site of today's MTA 207th Street Subway Yards, were at least partially reinterred at Woodlawn Cemetery in the early twentieth century. Meanwhile, the enslaved people of the local landowning families such as the Dyckmans, whose eighteenth-century house is now the Dyckman Farmhouse Museum, were buried within a hill at what is now 212th Street. Contractors came upon the burial ground in 1903 when preparing for the 10th Avenue extension. Inwood's amateur archaeologists William Calver and Reginald Bolton briefly witnessed the uncovered burials before they were destroyed by the leveling of the hill.

Article II of the New York State Constitution of 1821 required that "no man of colour, unless he shall have been for three years a citizen of this state, and for one year next preceding any election, shall be seized and possessed of a freehold estate of the value of two hundred and fifty dollars," should be entitled to vote. For Black New Yorkers, home ownership represented a much greater freedom than mere economic comfort. The pigeonhole for racial classification was big enough to deny nuance or even accuracy. As Carla L. Peterson points out in her book *Black Gotham*, with respect to the "African" homeowners and leaseholders of Lower Manhattan's Collect Street (now Centre Street) in the early nineteenth century, their genetic mix included English, Dutch, Moroccan, Indian, Spanish and probably indigenous North and South American. Very few of the residents would have had firsthand knowledge of Africa, which in and of itself happens to be the continent with the most genetic diversity.

In the nineteenth century, the modus operandi of Black success was keenly observed and reported on by all sides of the city. Jeremiah G. Hamilton, a successful Black Wall Street broker who profited from the devastation caused by the Great Fire of New York in 1835, and whose house was broken into and his white wife accosted by a lynch mob during the Civil War Draft Riots of 1863, was commonly referred to by the New York press as the "Prince of Darkness." In *The Works of James McCune Smith*, a collection of published essays by the nineteenth-century slave turned abolitionist and physician and the first African American to attain a medical degree (his three degrees were from the University of Glasgow in 1837 due to racial discrimination from American universities), Smith writes:

> *Compare Sam Ward* [a famous white lobbyist] *with the only black millionaire in New York, I mean Jerry Hamilton; and it is plain that manhood is a "nobler ideal" than money. The former has illustrated his people and his country, the other has fled from his identity (to use the elegant phraseology Ethiop), like a dog with a tin kettle tied to his tail!*

Smith's grave at Cypress Hills Cemetery is marked by a sign indicating a person of historic note. Hamilton, who owned land and property in Manhattan, present-day Astoria and upstate New York, is interred at his family plot, purchased a year after the Draft Riots, at Green-Wood Cemetery. If it weren't for Shane White's 2016 book, *Prince of Darkness*, Wall Street's first Black millionaire would be largely forgotten by history.

The Black middle class, in spite of myriad complexities, inequities, prejudice and scrutiny, nevertheless grew significantly during the nineteenth century. The five-acre Seneca Village was founded in the mid-1820s in what is now the Upper West Side of Central Park. Predominantly African American with additional Irish and German residents, who, as a collective workforce, contributed to the local Croton reservoir, Seneca Village had a combination of poor and middle-class homes, a school, churches and burial grounds for its population of two to three hundred. Manhattan's Saint Michael's Episcopalian Church, whose parish reach extended to All Angels Church at Seneca Village, provided a burial ground that was in use until the 1851 city ordinance forbade burials south of Eighty-Sixth Street. This resulted in the still-active Saint Michael's Cemetery on the Astoria/East Elmhurst border in Queens.

Once the construction of Central Park was approved in 1853, the inhabitants of Seneca Village and over one thousand other people, including farmers and squatters in the soon-to-be-upturned area, were evacuated. The structures therein were demolished by 1857. The dead were most likely reinterred at Saint Michael's Cemetery, although predictably, not all of them. Workmen at Central Park uncovered two coffin burials in the late 1800s. In 2005, the Seneca Village Project archaeological dig deliberately avoided the suspected burial grounds as a mark of respect. What appeared to be grave shafts were located in the area of the former African Union Methodist Church.

Stevedore James Weeks was the first to purchase a plot of land in the area that would come to be known as Weeksville in modern-day Crown Heights in Brooklyn. The neighborhood survived for a century until the Great Depression of the 1930s. African Americans began purchasing land in the area as early as 1838. Weeksville was a light at the end of the Underground Railroad tunnel for some of those seeking refuge from slave states. It presented much safer and better economic prospects than the unpredictably violent, racist elements of Manhattan that culminated in the Anti-Abolitionist Riots of 1834 and the Draft Riots of 1863. The crush of new European immigrants who came to New York in the nineteenth century added to the challenges of a city that placed African Americans at the bottom of the pecking order. Meanwhile, slavecatchers, in pursuit of slaves who had escaped from the South, were known to indulge in kidnapping—or blackbirding—by bundling free Black residents of the North off to the slave plantations of the South. The final post–Civil War Reconstruction Amendment—the Fifteenth Amendment of 1870—gave voting rights to male U.S. citizens who "shall not be denied or abridged by the United States or by any State on account of race, color, or previous condition of servitude." On May 14, 1870, the *New York Times* reported that the "Large Registration of Colored Voters" included one

Left: Weeksville Heritage Center in Crown Heights, Brooklyn.

Opposite: Fisk's patent airtight metallic burial cases. *Public domain.*

William Reece of Delancey Street "who is one hundred and eight years of age, and is yet in possession of all his faculties."

A fraction of the bucolic middle-class Weeksville houses that still stand are curated by the Weeksville Heritage Center. Weeksville's Citizens' Union Cemetery—later the Mount Pleasant Cemetery—was active from 1851 until it was sold in 1872 due to financial difficulty. The relocation of the dead to a designated plot at Cypress Hills Cemetery was reported to be a messy affair due to unrecorded identities and bodies dumped as refuse in the confusion. As is the case for so many New York cemetery transfers, it is probable that some of the dead were left behind.

In October 2011, construction workers uncovered a body in the area of Corona Avenue in Elmhurst, Queens, surrounded by fragments of what appeared to be an iron coffin. Thought to be a possible crime scene, a forensic anthropologist from the Medical Examiner's Office was called to the site. It was determined that the remains were of a five-foot, three-inch-tall young Black woman, aged somewhere between mid- and late twenties. Her overall preservation—including her long hair, a shroud, bonnet and stockings—was remarkable, especially considering that she probably died in the 1850s. The visible lesions on her preserved skin strongly indicated that smallpox was the cause of her death. A medical researcher from the Centers for Disease Control and Prevention in Atlanta confirmed that due to the absence of moisture and DNA in the woman's body, smallpox did not present the threat of a biohazard. Further research confirmed that an African American cemetery belonging to the United African Society—later the Saint Mark African Methodist Episcopal Church—had existed on the Elmhurst site during the nineteenth century. The relocation of the church to nearby Jackson Heights had left behind some of its cemetery's residents.

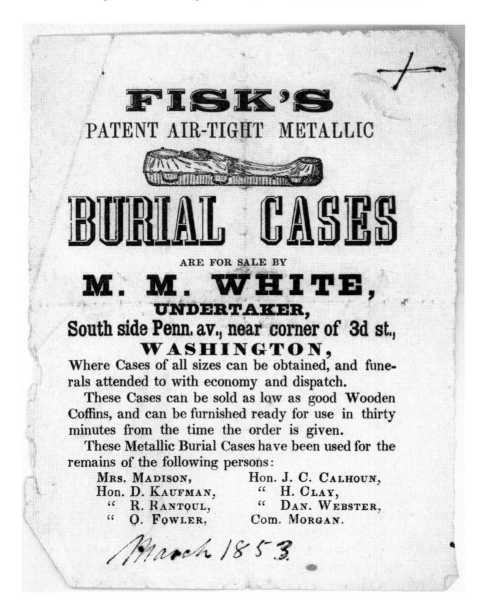

On November 14, 1848, a Manhattan stove designer, Almond Dunbar Fisk, received a patent for his "metallic burial case": an airtight iron coffin designed to accommodate the preservation of bodies on long-distance train travel in an era before embalming and refrigeration. Fisk & Raymond, the casket company that Almond Fisk ran with his father-in-law, became popular when former first lady Dolley Madison was buried in one of their Egyptian sarcophagus-style iron caskets, which often had a draped aesthetic and a window over the head of the deceased. As well as the Fisk & Raymond Broadway showroom, Fisk's foundry was in Newtown on Long Island, now the Woodside area of Queens. The local Fisk Avenue, now Sixty-Ninth Street, and the 69 St–Fisk Av station on the 7 train IRT Flushing line were named after the foundry.

The 1850 Newtown census provided a perfect fit for the woman in the iron coffin. An African American woman named Martha Peterson, aged twenty-six, was listed as a domestic worker living in the household of William Raymond, Almond Fisk's brother-in-law and neighbor, who had taken over the business following Fisk's death that same year. In addition to her personal connection to the iron coffin makers, Peterson's highly infectious smallpox would have been the main reason for her airtight iron coffin burial.

In 2016, after five years of research, the Saint Mark AME Church hired the Cushnie-Houston Funeral Home to organize Martha Peterson's twenty-first-century funeral arrangements. Peterson was reinterred, this time in a mahogany casket, at the nonsectarian Cemetery Belt fixture that is Mount Olivet in Maspeth, Queens. The burial ground, incorporated in 1850, contains approximately twenty reinterments from the site of the original Elmhurst cemetery where Martha Peterson's remains were discovered. Due to her assumed identity status, she is listed in the cemetery records as "Unknown," and perhaps as a consequence, there is currently no marker. Since the woman in the iron coffin's discovery, the Elmhurst History and Cemeteries Preservation Society has submitted a Request for Evaluation to the Landmarks Preservation Commission regarding the Elmhurst burial site, where other remains are presumed to be.

Steps toward ending racial discrimination during the late nineteenth century were taken tentatively, perhaps with the exception of the all-welcoming Bleeker Street dive bar called the Black and Tan (the owner Frank Stephenson is also credited with opening the city's first openly gay bar in the 1890s, called the Slide). Prominent cemeteries in New York City had their "colored" grounds and lots. Due to the evolving prejudices of the twentieth century, Black-owned or managed cemeteries such as Frederick Douglass Memorial Park in Oakwood, Staten Island, and funeral homes like Harlem's Benta Funerals Inc. served a need beyond death. Funeral director George Bernard Benta, who organized the funerals of some of the best-known Harlem-affiliated artists and activists, including Paul Robeson, Langston Hughes and James Baldwin, was a major driving force in the success of the ongoing four-generation-run funeral home. Benta, who died aged ninety-one in 2013, is interred at Woodlawn Cemetery in the Bronx with many of those whose funerals he arranged.

Founded in 1863 at what was then the southern end of Westchester, the four-hundred-acre Woodlawn Cemetery has the largest collection of mausoleums in America. Notwithstanding its appeal as a Gilded Age cemetery, the major draw for Woodlawn's regular visitors is its "Jazz Corner." Duke Ellington selected a spot for his family by a linden tree and was buried there in 1974. Other jazz musicians followed suit by purchasing plots nearby, including Miles Davis, Max Roach, Lionel Hampton and Jean-Baptiste "Illinois" Jacquet. The acclaimed jazz musicianship extends to Flushing Cemetery in Queens, where Dizzy Gillespie and Louis Armstrong are interred.

In Joseph Mitchell's essay "Mr. Hunter's Grave," written for the *New Yorker* and first published in 1956, eighty-seven-year-old Sandy Ground resident George Hunter, the son of a Virginia slave and a retiree from his successful cesspool building and cleaning business, expresses his concern regarding the shrinking space of Staten Island's AME Zion Cemetery. "It's a small cemetery," he said, "and we've been burying in it a long time, and it's getting crowded, and there's generations yet to come, and it worries me. Since I'm the chairman of the board of trustees, I'm in charge of selling graves in here, graves and plots, and I always try to encourage families to bury two to a grave."

Following the 1938 death of his second wife, Edith, Hunter asked the local gravedigger to dig an eight-foot-deep grave big enough for Edith and then him when the time came. Hunter also had his name and birth date etched into the grave marker under Edith's name. The gravedigger, however, either forgetful or work-shy, dug no more than six feet, and so when George

Hunter died at the age of ninety-seven in 1967, he was buried with his first wife, Celia Ann, whose remains lie in the Hunter plot adjacent to wife number two. Consequently, Mr. Hunter's death date was never added to the original marker. The makeshift circumstances of his burial make a touching, tragicomic epilogue to Joseph Mitchell's essay written a decade earlier, in which Hunter charms Mitchell with stories

Duke Ellington's grave at the "Jazz Corner" of Woodlawn Cemetery in the Bronx. *Hermis Pena/The Woodlawn Cemetery & Conservancy.*

Rossville AME Zion Church Cemetery in Staten Island.

of the history and neighborhood characters of Sandy Ground, a community within the neighborhood of Staten Island's Rossville.

In 1828, one year after slavery was abolished in New York State, ferry captain John Jackson became the first African American to purchase land on Staten Island. Sandy Ground, as it was colloquially known, is one of the oldest African American communities in the United States and was the first free community of its kind to establish itself in an area that would later be incorporated into New York City.

In the mid-nineteenth century, the Sandy Ground population grew to include a Maryland contingent fleeing racist state legislation. Others arriving from Virginia, Delaware and New Jersey contributed to and refined the community's main trade of oyster harvesting. Two centuries later, with that particular trade long-dead due to early twentieth-century water pollution in Raritan Bay, some of the descendants of the original Sandy Ground founders continue to live in the community. The local history museum is run by the Sandy Ground Historical Society while the Rossville AME Zion Cemetery, established in 1852, and its corresponding church, have been designated New York City landmarks. Tucked behind a fence on a quiet suburban street, the cemetery stands out from the other older African American graveyards of New York City due to its intact condition and the fact that it hasn't been forgotten or rediscovered.

6

AFFLICTIONS ARE THE STEPS TO HEAVEN

In 1889, a Roman Catholic nun named Frances Xavier Cabrini from Lombardy in Italy arrived in New York at the behest of Pope Leo XIII to help the large influx of poor Italian immigrants. After dedicating nearly thirty years of her life to founding multiple schools, orphanages and hospitals in New York and Chicago, she died in 1917 at the age of sixty-seven. Mother Cabrini became the first U.S. citizen to be canonized as a saint in 1946. Her prerequisite beatification miracle was to restore the sight of a baby, who, perhaps motivated by gratitude, grew up to be a priest. In 1950, a century after her birth, Mother Cabrini was named the patron saint of immigrants. Leading up to her canonization, her body was exhumed from her grave in Ulster County, New York, and divided. Her head was sent to Rome; her heart to Codogno, also in Italy; a bone from her arm found its way to her national shrine in Chicago; and the rest of her was incorporated into a wax face mask and hands and placed in a Snow White–style glass coffin at the Saint Frances Xavier Cabrini Shrine in Upper Manhattan's Washington Heights.

Another American saint, interred in one whole piece in a Maryland shrine, brings together the strands of prominent New York families of Dutch, British and French Huguenot descent, in and around the area of Lower Manhattan's Barclay Street.

The 1788 Doctors' Riot that began at Dr. Richard Bayley's makeshift laboratory at the New York Hospital building occurred six blocks north of the east end of Barclay Street. Connecticut-born Bayley, a physician, Columbia

Saint Frances Xavier Cabrini Shrine in Washington Heights, Manhattan. *St. Francis Xavier Cabrini Shrine NYC.*

College professor and leader in the field of epidemiology, cofounded the New York City Dispensary, authored the 1799 Quarantine Act and became the first health officer for the Port of New York, a position that led to his death from yellow fever in 1801. Bayley's first wife, Catherine Charlton, was the daughter of Reverend Richard Charlton—rector for the first Anglican parish on Staten Island, now the Church of Saint Andrew in Richmondtown. Bayley, Charlton and his daughter Catherine are buried in its churchyard.

In 1778, a year after Catherine took ill and died, Dr. Bayley married his second wife, Charlotte Barclay, who became stepmother to his two young daughters Elizabeth and Catherine. Together they had two sons, Guy and Richard. Charlotte was the daughter of a Roosevelt and the sister-in-law of a Van Cortlandt. Her sister, Catherine, married Augustus Frederickszen Cortlandt, great-grandson of Dutch brewer Oloff Stevensz Van Cortlandt, after whom Cortlandt Street, which is four blocks south of Barclay Street, is named. Charlotte was the granddaughter of Reverend Thomas Barclay who established Albany's first Anglican parish, now the New York State capital's Saint Peter's Episcopal Church. Thomas's son and Charlotte's uncle, Reverend Henry Barclay, was the second rector of Trinity Church, which is seven blocks south of Barclay Street, from 1746 to 1764. He is buried in its churchyard, and Barclay Street was named in his honor. Charlotte, who separated from Dr. Bayley, is buried at Vault Hill Cemetery, otherwise known as the Van Cortlandt Burial Ground in Van Cortlandt Park in the Bronx.

When Dr. Bayley's eldest daughter, Elizabeth, reached nineteen, she married William Magee Seton, the son of a wealthy Scottish merchant who worked at his father's mercantile firm. Together they had five children and attended Trinity Church. When William died in 1803 in Italy, where they had gone to seek a warmer climate for his tuberculosis, Elizabeth was introduced to Catholicism. The resultant shift in her worldview was profound. She returned to New York and on March 14, 1805, converted to Catholicism at Saint Peter's Roman Catholic Church on Barclay Street. She later founded the first American congregation of religious sisters, the Sisters of Charity, and the first free Catholic school for girls in the United States in Emmitsburg, Maryland.

Elizabeth and members of her family were crucial figures in the molding of nineteenth-century Catholic America. Her daughter Catherine would become the first American adoptee of the Dublin-founded Sisters of Mercy when it branched out across the Atlantic, and her nephew James, the son of her half brother Guy Carlton Bayley, the grandson of Dr. Richard and Charlotte Bayley and a cousin of both future Roosevelt presidents, was ordained as a priest at Manhattan's Saint Patrick's Cathedral before filling the positions of the first bishop of Newark and then archbishop of Baltimore.

In 1975, 154 years after her death, Elizabeth Ann Seton became the first American-born saint. She is interred, along with her nephew, Archbishop James Roosevelt Bayley, at the National Shrine of Elizabeth Ann Seton in Emmitsburg, Maryland. The New York City Shrine of Saint Elizabeth Ann Bayley Seton is located in Manhattan's Financial District in the Church of Our Lady of the Holy Rosary. Elizabeth's grandson and James's cousin Robert Seton was the first person in the United States to receive the high ranking of "Prelatura" and then prothonotary apostolic clergy status in the 1860s. He was also the rector of Jersey City's Saint Joseph's Church, the dean of all monsignori throughout the nation, and to top it all off, in 1903, he was bestowed the time immemorial position of the titular archbishop of Heliopolis in Phoenicia.

Both James and Elizabeth's conversion to Catholicism shocked and offended members of their family and community alike. When Saint Peter's Roman Catholic Church, at which Saint Elizabeth converted, was established in 1785, the American republic was brand new. The Bill of Rights and the First Amendment that ensured the protection of free speech and religious practice was six years away. Due to widespread anti-Catholic bias, the church was situated outside the city limits at today's Barclay and

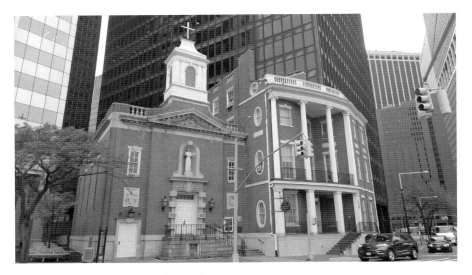

Shrine of Saint Elizabeth Ann Bayley Seton in Lower Manhattan.

Church Streets. The parish and its accompanying churchyard were the first Catholic church and cemetery in New York State.

An excerpt from a report written a century earlier in 1687 by New York governor Thomas Dongan to the Lords of Trade and Plantations, reads:

> *Every town ought to have a Minister. New York has first a Chaplain belonging to the Fort of the Church of England; secondly, a Dutch Calvinist; thirdly a French Calvinist; fourthly a Dutch Lutheran. Here be not many of the Church of England; a few Roman Catholics; abundance of Quaker preachers, men and women especially. Singing Quakers, Ranting Quakers, Sabbatarians, Antisabbatarians, some Anabaptists, some independents, some Jews; in short of all sorts of opinions there are some, and the most part of none at all.*

In the first of his five years in office, Dongan, from County Kildare, the second Earl of Limerick and the first Catholic governor of New York, put together the Charter of Liberties and Privileges, which was passed in 1683 by the newly formed New York General Assembly. The charter established the government's place and lawful procedures within the colony and the liberties of the individuals therein. It wasn't to last. In the last decade of the seventeenth century, New York officials were forced to swear oaths against the Catholic Church in the wake of Britain's war with Catholic Spain. In spite of the small Catholic population, in 1700 their religion was banned, and Catholic priests were forbidden from entering the New York colony.

In the late eighteenth century, German Jesuit missionary Ferdinand Steinmeyer, also known as Father Farmer, risked death and incarceration by preaching to clandestine gatherings in private Manhattan homes. The Catholic ban was repealed in 1784 after the end of the Revolution. The mixed parish from Ireland, Germany, France and Mediterranean Europe moved fast to establish an official place of worship with the help of an Irish Capuchin friar, Father Charles Whelan. Shortly after the end of the Revolutionary War, with the British forces gone from the city, donations including one thousand silver pieces from King Charles III of Spain aided the construction of Saint Peter's Catholic Church. The first free Catholic school in New York State, Saint Peter's Free School, would follow in 1800.

In the early hours of Christmas Day 1806, a riot broke out at the church when a gang of roughly fifty anti-Catholic nativists called the Highbinders targeted the congregation. One of the city's watchmen, Christian Luswanger, was stabbed to death in the ensuing violence and is listed as the first New York police officer to be killed in the line of duty. In an additional footnote to reckless crime, Saint Peter's claims to be in possession of records that verify the church baptism of one Henry McCarty on September 28, 1859. Twenty years later, McCarty would shoot his way into outlaw history as Billy the Kid.

A larger Greek Revival church was completed in 1838 on the site of the old Saint Peter's. During construction, graves from its churchyard were reinterred at an additional burial ground, purchased in 1801, and situated farther north. This second Catholic cemetery in today's Nolita neighborhood would become the site of New York's first Saint Patrick's Cathedral—now the Basilica of Saint Patrick's Old Cathedral—and the seat of the first bishop of the Diocese of New York. Designed by Joseph Mangin in the Gothic Revival style, it was the largest cathedral in the United States upon its completion in 1815. Apart from the crypts of Catholic clergy in the current Saint Patrick's Cathedral on Fifth Avenue, the basilica's crypts and burial ground constitute the only remaining Catholic cemetery in Manhattan. Due to its former cathedral status, the church was declared a minor basilica by Pope Benedict XVI on Saint Patrick's Day, 2010.

The high brick wall around the basilica, equipped with peephole views of the cemetery within its gates, was built as a fort in the early 1830s for protection against nativist anti-Catholic gangs and organizations whose intent was to burn the cathedral to the ground. Consequently, the Ancient Order of the Hibernians, a nineteenth-century Irish American fraternal organization much-practiced in defending its territory, had headquarters nearby. Following architect Henry Englebert's restoration of the cathedral after an accidental fire in 1866, it reopened in 1868 and continued as a cathedral until the consecration of the new Saint Patrick's on Fifth Avenue in 1879, which took twenty-one years to complete.

Burials at the Basilica of Saint Patrick's Old Cathedral that were later reinterred at Saint Patrick's Cathedral include Ulster-born Archbishop John Hughes—otherwise known as Dagger John because of his abrasive nature and the dagger-shaped cross he incorporated into his signature—and Pierre Toussaint, who was brought to New York from the French colony of Saint-Domingue as a slave in 1787. Freed at the age of forty-five in 1807 upon the death of his mistress Madame Bérard, Pierre became a successful hairdresser to wealthy clients and took the name Toussaint in honor of the Revolutionary Haitian hero Toussaint Louverture, who had liberated Pierre's birthplace. Along with his wife, Juliette Noel, a woman whose freedom he had purchased, Pierre Toussaint immersed himself in charity that included opening an orphanage and raising money to build the first Saint Patrick's Cathedral.

In 1996, Toussaint was declared "Venerable" by Pope John Paul II and is currently being investigated by the Vatican for possible canonization. Toussaint died in 1853 at the age of eighty-seven and was buried alongside Juliette and their adopted daughter at Old Saint Patrick's. Reinterred at the new Saint Patrick's, Toussaint became the first layperson to be buried in the crypt below the main altar.

The grave of John Dubois, from Paris, the third bishop of the Roman Catholic Diocese of New York and also the first non-Irish-born bishop, who provided spiritual guidance for Saint Elizabeth Ann Seton, sits just outside the entrance to the basilica. Before he died, Dubois's burial request was thus: "Bury me where the people walk over me in death as they wished to in life."

On August 21, 1879, fifteen people including a boy named John Curry, aged five or six, claimed to have witnessed the apparition of the Virgin Mary flanked by the impressive company of St. Joseph and St. John the Evangelist in Knock, County Mayo, in the west of Ireland. Curry later moved to New York, where he became a hospital attendant. When he died in 1943, he was buried in an unmarked grave at Farmingdale, Long Island. In 2017, however, it was decided that Curry, the last visionary of the miracle at what is now Ireland's pilgrimage site of Knock Shrine (or the Sanctuary of Our Lady of Knock), would be reinterred at the Basilica.

Others buried at the basilica include Francis Delmonico of the famous restaurateur Delmonico family; "Honest John" Kelly, who, as the boss of Tammany Hall took on the corruption left behind by his predecessor, William "Boss" Tweed; and actor John "Cha Cha" Ciarcia, also known as the "Mayor of Little Italy." Ciarcia's Little Italy restaurant, Cha Cha's In Bocca Al Lupo Café, was frequented by Manhattan's Italian American movie elite, many of whom were familiar with the basilica. Both Francis Ford Coppola and Martin Scorsese used the basilica and its churchyard as film locations for *The Godfather* and *Mean Streets*, respectively.

Scorsese, a former Saint Patrick's Old Cathedral altar boy, has a mausoleum in the picturesque Moravian Cemetery in New Dorp, Staten Island, in which his parents are interred and where he will one day join them. Active since 1740, Moravian Cemetery is the largest and oldest cemetery on Staten Island and was built to accommodate the Protestant Moravian Church and its original congregation of early eighteenth-century Czech settlers. Part of the 113 cemetery acres was donated by the well-heeled Dutch American industrialists the Vanderbilt family, who have their own Frederick Law Olmsted–designed private section within the cemetery grounds. In the early twentieth century, Italian immigrants were gathered together by an Italian mission that conducted services at the Moravian church, which is why Moravian Cemetery,

Scorsese mausoleum at Moravian Cemetery in Staten Island.

now nonsectarian, is the burial place for so many Italian American Catholics. Moravian Cemetery resident and son of Italian immigrants Paul "Big Paulie" Castellano, the head of the Gambino crime family before he was assassinated in 1985 on the orders of his successor John Gotti, was refused a Catholic funeral by the Archdiocese of New York for a list of sins that would take far longer to recite than the most meticulous eulogy.

Contrary to popular belief, it is still possible to be buried in Lower Manhattan so long as one can afford it. A full family crypt at the Basilica of Saint Patrick's Old Cathedral was made available in 2016 for an astounding $7 million, with the option to subdivide it into individual coffin space starting at $850,000. To raise extra income for the upkeep of the complex, the basilica, like a good handful of Manhattan churches, has been offering cremation niches in the underground catacombs that sell for $10,000 to $15,000 each. The Catholic Church lifted the ban on cremation in 1963, and since 1966, funeral rites are permitted so long as the ashes are committed to cemeteries and columbariums (derived from the Latin *columba*—for pigeon, meaning "pigeon-house") owned and run by Catholic parishes and dioceses.

In 1841, when a pre-archbishop John Hughes was a mere coadjutor bishop, he founded the first Catholic institution for higher learning in the northeastern United States. Saint John's College, now Fordham University in the Bronx, a private research university and the third-oldest university in New York State after Columbia and New York Universities, is in possession of its own cemetery. Established in 1847, it took approximately four decades for the burial ground to get in the way of the construction plans for the New York Botanical Garden. A new cemetery was established soon after, next to the college church where most of the old burials were reinterred. The last burial at the newer ground took place in 1909, and the majority of the 138 college-affiliated graves belong to Jesuits.

Three of the Jesuits were reinterred at Saint Raymond's Cemetery in the Bronx neighborhood of Throggs Neck, on land purchased by Bishop John Hughes. Present-day Saint Raymond's Old and New Cemeteries sit on 180 acres, the latter of which is the borough's only active Catholic burial ground. The Whittemore Avenue gates of the Old Cemetery, established in 1875, were the 1932 drop-off point for the $50,000 ransom paid to the kidnappers of Charles Lindbergh's ill-fated baby son. The Old Cemetery includes the Celtic Cross grave of "Fighting 69th" Regiment World War I priest and battlefield hero Father Francis Patrick Duffy (whose fist-clenched statue stands before another Celtic Cross at Times Square) and the gray granite headstone of "Typhoid Mary" Mallon.

An asymptomatic typhoid-carrying cook, Mallon, from County Tyrone in what is now Northern Ireland, infected seven of the eight New York families she cooked for within the first seven years of the twentieth century. After a three-year quarantine on North Brother Island in the East River, during which time the majority of her typhoid samples tested positive, Mallon was released on the condition that she no longer cook professionally. Fully aware that cooking paid a higher wage than other domestic work, Mallon used assumed names and carried on cooking, this time at Sloane Hospital for Women. When twenty-five staff and patients at the hospital became infected, two of whom died, Mallon fled to Long Island, where she was eventually captured. She was promptly marched back to North Brother Island, where she spent the remaining twenty-three years of her life. Her body is alleged to have been cremated in 1938 as a safety precaution, in which case her ashes were buried in a Catholic cemetery twenty-five years before the Catholic Church lifted its ban on cremation.

The separated old and new segments of Saint Raymond's are similar to Staten Island's oldest Roman Catholic burial ground, Saint Peter's Cemetery, established in 1848. The older parts of both cemeteries are overwhelmingly Irish and largely populated by the great exodus from Ireland's Great Famine in the 1840s. At Saint Peter's, some of the oldest Irish graves are carved with the deceased person's county of origin.

Saint Raymond's New Cemetery, active since 1953, a decade before the Old Cemetery reached full capacity, has a uniform aesthetic from its parade of thigh-high marble markers to the New World Catholic sheen of its towering community mausoleums, gold motifs, saintly mosaics and tinkling fountains. The graves of troubled music icons Billie Holiday, La Lupe and Frankie Lymon are decorated with tributes.

Saint Raymond's cemeteries, along with Calvary Cemetery in Queens, Resurrection Cemetery in Staten Island and two more cemeteries in Upstate New York, are owned and operated by the Archdiocese of New York. Calvary was consecrated in 1848 by John Hughes two years before he became the archbishop of New York. Managed by the trustees of Saint Patrick's Cathedral, Calvary takes up 365 acres of the northwesterly section of the Cemetery Belt. By the early nineteenth century, Saint Patrick's Old Cathedral Cemetery and another Catholic burial ground at Eleventh Street were already running out of space, so in 1845, the trustees purchased seventy-one acres of land in Maspeth, Long Island, in the present-day borough of Queens. The Alsop family sold their farmland to Saint Patrick's as additional cemetery space, on the condition that their private burial

Grave of Billie Holiday at St. Raymond New Cemetery in the Bronx.

plot would remain, which it did and still does. Like many of the mid-nineteenth-century New York cemeteries, Calvary was accessible by ferry from Manhattan. A popular filming location, it has appeared in *Midnight Cowboy* and *The Godfather*.

The four sections of Calvary, formally named St. Callixtus, St. Agnes, St. Sebastian and St. Domitilla, after four of the ancient Roman catacombs, make up the largest cemetery (by the number of interments) in the United States with approximately three million residents. Each of the cemetery divisions demonstrates the timeline of Catholic migration to New York City from Ireland, Germany, Italy and Latin America. The Old Calvary section, in possession of the best postcard view of the Manhattan skyline, received its first burial on July 31, 1848, after Esther Ennis died of "a broken heart." Atop a Calvary hill is the elegant mausoleum of the fantastically bawdy Texas Guinan, the descendant of Irish immigrants. After making her name as a silent film star, she became better known as the "Queen of the Nightclubs" for her fast-talking Manhattan speakeasy hostess skills during Prohibition. At the age of forty-nine, she contracted amoebic dysentery from an outbreak in a Chicago hotel and died one month before the end of Prohibition in 1933. On her deathbed she declared, "I would rather have a square inch of New York than all the rest of the world."

By the mid-nineteenth century, Irish-born immigrants made up a quarter of New York City's population. In 1863, the New York City Parks

Calvary Cemetery in Queens.

Department purchased a plot of land at Calvary from the trustees as a burial place for fallen Union soldiers. Among those buried there is Sligo-born commander of the all-Irish Sixty-Ninth Regiment, Michael Corcoran, about whom songs have been written and whose death was caused by a runaway horse that threw him off its back in Fairfax in 1863.

Section three of Calvary embodies the Italian migrants whose numbers in New York accelerated to over two million during the first decade of the twentieth century. Their combined presence made an indelible mark on the city's culture. Meanwhile, the Sicilian mafia enveloped itself in America's underbelly while adding colorful footnotes to the changing shape of New York City. Sicilian Black Hand gang leader Ignazio Lupo, otherwise known as Lupo the Wolf, shares his brother-in-law's plot in Calvary's third section beneath an unassuming headstone. Suspected of dozens of murders, Lupo's New York gang merger resulted in the city's all-powerful Morello crime family. Close by, the bust of Lupo's investigator, Detective Joseph Petrosino, perched high on a grave pillar, keeps a watchful eye over the cemetery. A pioneer in fighting organized crime, Petrosino became the first person in NYPD history to be murdered on duty outside of the United States during his investigation of the mafia in Sicily in 1909. He was also responsible for warning the Secret Service of an impending assassination attempt on President McKinley in 1901. Upon his visit to the Pan-American Exposition in Buffalo in western New York, McKinley chose to ignore the warning. As

Roadside plaque in remembrance of President William McKinley's assassination in Buffalo, New York.

a result, the plaque that marks the place of his assassination resides in the middle of an island on a suburban Buffalo street.

If Calvary Cemetery were to have just one representative, it may as well be Annie Moore, whose unmarked grave was only identified in 2006. Prior to becoming the first person to be processed through Ellis Island in 1892, which had just replaced Castle Clinton in Manhattan's Battery Park as New York State's immigration registration station, she would have sailed past the welcoming sonnet of "The New Colossus" on the base of the Statue of Liberty pedestal, penned by Emma Lazarus, who is buried less than five miles away. Moore arrived in New York City at the age of seventeen aboard a steamship called *Nevada*. When Annie died from heart failure in 1924 at the age of forty-seven, she was so large that she had to be lifted out of the window of her home by a team of firefighters. Two statues of Annie, sculpted by Jeanne Rynhart, stand at Cobh Heritage Centre in County Cork in Ireland and at Ellis Island, her ports of departure and arrival.

Brooklyn's Cathedral Basilica of Saint James dates back to 1822, making it the oldest Catholic parish and cemetery on Long Island and the third oldest in the boroughs that compose present-day New York City. The establishment of the Roman Catholic Diocese of Brooklyn in 1853 allowed the parish to acquire cathedral status. In the 1980s, the status of Saint James was elevated once again to a Minor Papal Basilica. In 1849, the year in which cholera decimated New York City and the surrounding counties, Brooklyn, then an independent city, had its own ban on inner-city burials, putting an end to Saint James's churchyard activity. The present-day basilica in Downtown Brooklyn, erected in 1903, covers some of the estimated seven thousand interments.

In the New York City region, Catholic Cemeteries of the Roman Catholic Diocese of Brooklyn control Most Holy Trinity Cemetery in Brooklyn and Saint Monica and Our Lady of Mount Carmel Cemeteries in Queens. In 2007, the Brooklyn Diocese handed over control of Holy Cross Cemetery in Brooklyn and Saint John and Mount Saint Mary Cemeteries in Queens to Saint John's Cemetery Corporation. The domain of the latter organization, Saint John Cemetery, in the Cemetery Belt area of Middle Village, Queens, is a who's who of twentieth-century New York crime and politics. The atmosphere and décor of the Saint John Cloister community mausoleum has the air of a business hotel between bookings. Its residents include three-term governor of New York Mario Cuomo and crime bosses John Gotti and Carlo Gambino. Additional mafioso Salvatore "Lucky Luciano" Lucania has his own mausoleum, while on the easterly fringes of the cemetery, Robert Mapplethorpe, known among other things for his BDSM photography, lies low beneath a simple block headstone.

Most Holy Trinity in Brooklyn's Bushwick neighborhood is a strong contender for the Cemetery Belt's most unique segment. Developed in

1851 for the German Catholic parish of Most Holy Trinity Church in East Williamsburg, its twenty-three-acres, purchased from next door's Evergreen Cemetery, grew to accommodate twenty-five thousand interments, including reinterments from the old Most Holy churchyard. To demonstrate that there is no hierarchy in death, the humble materials of tin, and to a lesser degree wood and copper, add up to a creaking array of grave markers. Some of the tin markers look like vandalized postboxes, ripped and gaping open. Rusty, ionized crosses supporting crucified Jesus figures resemble a Christian tribute to antiquated plumbing. Religious statues with severed hollow arms, stooped and sinking into the earth, look less saintly than accident-prone. All of this is scored by the L train running along the cemetery's western border.

Statue grave marker at Most Holy Trinity Cemetery in Brooklyn.

Left: Cross grave marker at Most Holy Trinity Cemetery in Brooklyn.

Right: Christogram symbol.

Among the commonplace symbols in Catholic cemeteries are the letters IHS or IHC from the first lower-case Greek letters (*iota*, *eta*, *sigma*), for Jesus. When the IHS letters are superimposed over one another, they resemble the dollar sign. Another is the Chi-Rho symbol, a monogram of X and P, the first two Greek capital letters for Christ—*Christos*—used by Emperor Constantine as an early Christogram on his military flag and on the shields of his army. The *chi* letter is also where the festive abbreviation *Xmas* comes from. K of C can be found on the tombstones and emblems of the Knights of Columbus, with a medieval knight's shield mounted on a formée cross. Early on, the fraternal organization, whose members have included John F. Kennedy, Jeb Bush and Babe Ruth, provided financial assistance to the widows and orphans of its members. Founded in New Haven, Connecticut, in 1882, the Knights of Columbus have often been described as the "Catholic Masons," encouraged by the papal ban of Freemasonry and other secret societies in 1738. Their antiabortion stance is on view outside an increasing number of parishes in the shape of a "Tomb of the Unborn Child" headstone.

The newer sections of active Catholic cemeteries represent twentieth- and twenty-first-century shifts in migration from United States territories, Latin America, the Caribbean, Europe, Africa and Asia. The Immigration and Nationality Act of 1965 changed the demographics by putting an end

Knights of Columbus abortion memorial at St. Peter's Cemetery in West Brighton, Staten Island.

to the previous racially biased quota system. Additionally, when the Bracero Program—created by the government as a World War II–era agricultural California workforce and composed of poorly paid and discriminated-against Mexican migrants—ended in 1964, Mexican migration traveled north. Of the combined practiced religions, Catholicism is now the dominant religion of New York City at around 60 percent. Saint Elizabeth Ann Seton's popular quote, "Afflictions are the steps to heaven," can perhaps sum up the perseverance of Catholic New York, which has come a long way from its early days of clandestine minority gatherings.

7

CRIME, PUNISHMENT AND INVESTIGATION

On Friday the thirteenth in July 1860, Albert Hicks, nicknamed the "last pirate of New York," became, as his moniker suggests, the last person to be executed for piracy in the state of New York. After murdering the three-man crew of an oyster sloop, the *A.E. Johnson*, with an axe for the purpose of stealing a large bundle of cash, Hicks threw the bodies of evidence overboard but left behind a few stubborn, careless digits on the bloodstained deck—more precisely, four fingers and a thumb.

In the aftermath of getting caught and making his confession, Hicks was escorted to Bedloe's Island—today's Liberty Island. Its waterside geography fell into the traditional site for pirate executions. Although this wasn't officially a public execution, an event that had been outlawed a quarter of a century earlier, the hanging of Albert Hicks nevertheless drew an estimated twelve thousand spectators on stuffed pleasure steamers and anchored boats, including the freshly mopped and painted *A.E. Johnson*, the scene of the crime for the last pirate of New York. Some of those witnesses may have heard Hicks's last words: "Hang me quick—make haste." Earlier that same year, in April 1860, New York governor Edwin D. Morgan signed a bill to repeal hanging. Without a viable replacement, capital punishment was accidentally abolished in the state of New York. Albert Hicks nevertheless missed any inadvertent outcome, and the death penalty was officially reinstated in 1861.

The old English penal laws traveled with the early American colonists as old habits tend to do. Puritan New England showed little mercy for so-called crimes against morality and went as far as executing the animals subjected to the crime of bestiality along with the human perpetrator. Far less liberal and conciliatory than Dutch New Amsterdam, British colonial New York mingled the noose arrangement with the less common executions of fire at the stake and the breaking wheel.

The large turnout for the Albert Hicks execution was nothing new. Lured by curiosity and excitement, the same marketable appeal twirled its goods at ancient gladiatorial games. Killing in all its forms can so easily be peddled as a spectator's sport. Peeking at the great unknown, at those moments leading into the great abyss, has had us spellbound for the larger part of history. Deterrence and comeuppance were—and still are in parts of the world—the justifications for public execution. In New York, such reasoning eventually wore thin due to the gatherings often ending in public drunkenness and petty crime. The public was cordially encouraged to attend executions so that the power structure of the crown and then state, implemented between the gavel and the pen-pusher, could demonstrate exactly who was in charge, and who, ultimately, had the power and authority to inflict death without consequence. Concurrently, public execution allowed the voyeuristic impulses of the crowd to thrive without shame. After all, it was the criminals facing due punishment who were the real wrongdoers.

Resistance to capital punishment gained traction in the late eighteenth and nineteenth centuries when ruminations born out of the Enlightenment and the rising middle class produced particular sensitivities. Execution, the sick, the dying and the dead were moving further away from public life with the advent of hospitals and out-of-town cemeteries, thereby pushing a cultural shift toward introspection and a revised perspective on physical pain. The image of the condemned, put to death by a civilized society, reflected back increasingly unfavorably on its onlookers and participants. James Madison, Benjamin Rush, DeWitt Clinton and Horace Greeley were among those who used skepticism and compassion as tools with which to challenge the death sentence. By the mid-1830s, execution in New York State was transferred from a public to a private space.

As reported by the *Buffalo Evening News*, on the night of August 7, 1881, a man named Lemuel Smith, at the behest of a peccadillo that will forever remain unknown, entered the Brush Electric Company's arc lighting powerhouse. Ignoring the station manager's order to stay away from the dynamo, Smith returned a while later, grabbed the brushes of the electric generator with both hands and, unsurprisingly, dropped dead.

Buffalo local, scientific society member, former engineer and dentist Alfred Porter Southwick paid special attention to the news of the unfortunate incident and had a light bulb idea. Together with fellow Buffalo resident, surgeon and inventor George Fell, Southwick experimented with various electrocution techniques, including—somewhat ironically—the execution of stray dogs for the Buffalo branch of the American Society for the Prevention of Cruelty to Animals. Finally, Southwick decided that this particular death application, paired with his modified dentist's chair, would make a more humane method of capital punishment than common hanging.

Various methods of hanging, including the nineteenth-century American-invented upright jerker, which threw the condemned skyward through the use of weights and pulleys with the best laid plans of snapping the neck, had long proved inconsistent. The gamut of hanging techniques failed to prevent botched results with consequences ranging from slow strangulation to decapitation. Consequences of miscalculations ranged from slow strangulation to decapitation. Seventy-seven-year-old Oscar Beckwith, nicknamed the "Cannibal of Austerlitz" for—according to folklore—eating his victim in Upstate New York after a disagreement over a gold mine, was hanged for mere first-degree murder in Hudson's Columbia County Jail on March 1, 1888. Unfortunately for Beckwith, he swung for eighteen minutes before death relieved him of his motion sickness.

In response to Southwick and Fell's experiments, New York State governor David B. Hill set up the Gerry Commission. Formed with and named after the lawyer and human rights advocate Elbridge Thomas Gerry, the purpose of the commission was to conduct research and collect expert opinions based on Southwick's proposal. On June 4, 1888, the New York legislature enacted a law to replace hanging with electrocution that would go into effect on January 1, 1889. Henceforth, New York would become the first state to use the electric chair at Auburn and Sing Sing Prisons and to centralize its system of capital punishment.

A delay ensued, caused by the war of currents between Thomas Edison's direct current and George Westinghouse's alternating current, a war in which neither party wanted his electrical charge to be sullied by a death-inducing seat. The delay allowed for further old-school executions. On December 5, 1889, in Manhattan's prison, the Tombs, "Handsome Harry" Carlton, sentenced to death for the murder of a policeman, became the last person to be executed by hanging in New York City. The following day, at Brooklyn's Raymond Street Jail, John Greenwall, sentenced to death for murder and burglary, became the last person to be executed by hanging in New York State.

On August 6, 1890, after the Supreme Court had declared the electric chair to be constitutional and humane, William Kemmler, sentenced to death for murdering his girlfriend with a hatchet, was brought into the execution chamber at Auburn Prison in Central New York for what would be the first ever state-sanctioned killing using electricity. In front of more than twenty witnesses—men of medicine and science, clergymen, prison staff, law enforcement, press and electric chair champions Southwick and Fell—Kemmler was seated and strapped into a chair that had been surreptitiously monitored by Thomas Edison. Against the wishes of George Westinghouse and advantageous to Edison's desire to besmirch his opponent's reputation, the electric chair's power source relied on alternating current.

Kemmler was electrocuted for seventeen seconds. It is at this untimely moment that Southwick is reported to have confidently announced: "There is the culmination of ten years' work and study. We live in a higher civilization from this day." Southwick's proclamation would have been somewhat overshadowed by the fact that Kemmler was still alive and breathing heavily. To prevent a second failure, this time the current was turned on for a longer period of seventy seconds, although some witnesses claim that it was as long as four minutes. The *New York Times* described bleeding, an unbearable stench and the overall effect of the execution on the witnesses: "It had nauseated all but a few of them, and the sick ones had to be looked out for.…They all seemed to act as though they felt that they had taken part in a scene that would be told to the world as a public shame, as a legal crime."

Attending physician Dr. Carlos Frederick McDonald's report noted that Kemmler's visible distress after the first current was probably the result of "reflex muscular movement" and that "the second application of the current was maintained too long." McDonald concluded that compared with hanging, "execution by electricity is infinitely preferable." The victim of William Kemmler's hatchet crime, Matilda "Tillie" Ziegler, is buried in Buffalo's Forest Lawn Cemetery, where Alfred P. Southwick is also interred.

Although the first woman to die in the electric chair was Martha Place at Sing Sing in 1899 for the murder of her stepdaughter, the first woman ever to be sentenced to the electric chair was Lizzie Halliday in 1894. Originally from County Antrim in Ireland, Lizzy became a serial killer in the state of New York and was responsible for the deaths of a handful of people, including her husband. She was spared "Old Sparky," as the electric chair came to be known in many prisons, thanks to a diagnosis of criminal insanity. Instead, Lizzy was sent to the Matteawan State Hospital for the Criminally Insane in Beacon, New York, where in 1906, she fatally stabbed head attendant Nellie Wicks two hundred times with a pair of scissors.

On February 18, 1916, the electrocution of Hans Schmidt, a German Catholic priest convicted of killing and dismembering his housekeeper in

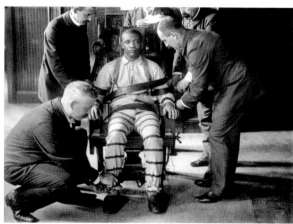

Above: Grave of Alfred Porter Southwick at Forest Lawn Cemetery in Buffalo, New York.

Left: Electric chair, a.k.a. "Old Sparky," at Sing-Sing; man identified as Arthur Mayhew, executed on March 12, 1897. *Public domain.*

Midtown Manhattan after discovering that she was pregnant with his child, took place in Sing Sing, making him the only Catholic priest ever to be executed in the United States.

In 1934, Francis Pasqua, Daniel Kreisberg, Tony Marino and Joseph Murphy were executed at Sing Sing for the murder of a homeless Irish alcoholic named Michael Malloy, from whom they had hoped to gain a life insurance payout in the event of his "accidental" death. Malloy's casual resistance to death, which usually occurred when he was already unconscious from booze, earned him the nicknames "Durable Mike," "Iron Mike" and "Rasputin of the Bronx." Malloy's liquored-up capacity for

Albert Fish mug shot, 1903. *Public domain.*

outwitting the grim reaper defied the plotters' multiple attempts at murder, which included poisoning, freezing and running him over with a car. Finally, Malloy succumbed to death from a gas jet hose pipe that was placed in his mouth as he lay passed out, drunk and oblivious.

On January 16, 1936, it was the turn of sixty-five-year-old Albert Fish, a child serial killer and cannibal nicknamed the "Brooklyn Vampire," to sit in Sing Sing's hot seat. While awaiting execution, Fish committed pen to paper in an attempt to list the details of his crimes, but his "filthy string of obscenities" were deemed unpublishable.

The seventy-three-year lifespan of the electric chair in New York State, where it was the only method of capital punishment starting in 1890, ended the lives of 686 men and 9 women. Eddie Lee Mays, who was sentenced to death for first-degree murder during the robbery of a bar in East Harlem, was the last person to be executed in New York State at Sing Sing on August 15, 1963. Lewis E. Lawes, the prison warden for Sing Sing between 1920 and 1941 and the author of a number of books, including *20,000 Years in Sing Sing*, upon which the 1932 film of the same name, starring Spencer Tracy, was based, supervised the electric chair executions of 303 prisoners. He posed the question, "Did you ever see a rich man go the whole route through to the Death House? I don't know of any." As a consequence of his undeniable experience in matters of death, Lawes opposed the death penalty. Alabama, Florida, Kentucky, South Carolina and Tennessee are the only places in the world where the New York State–invented electric chair is still in use, although it is optional alongside lethal injection.

On August 14, 1936, Rainey Bethea, who confessed to rape, murder and theft but was convicted of only rape, was publicly hanged in Owensboro,

Kentucky, in front of a crowd of twenty thousand. The combination of a visibly drunk hangman and the negative publicity that followed were instrumental in making it the last public execution in the United States.

On June 29, 1972, the death penalty was invalidated nationwide by the Supreme Court following *Furman v. Georgia*, a case involving burglar William Furman, whose shot in the dark killed the homeowner who had tried to apprehend him. A 5–4 ruling narrowly decided that capital punishment violated the Eighth and Fourteenth Amendments. The death penalty bounced back, however, with *Gregg v. Georgia* in 1976, when the Supreme Court, in a 7–2 majority, decided that sentencing hitchhiker murderer Troy Leon Gregg to death was indeed constitutional. Georgia, like thirty-six other states, had presented new statutes with amended sentencing guidelines and refined death penalty crime categories.

When Delaware native Bill Bailey was sentenced to death for the 1979 double murder of an elderly married couple, he chose hanging over lethal injection, stating, "I'm not going to let them put me to sleep." He was executed at Delaware Correctional Center on January 25, 1996, and was declared dead eleven minutes after the rope around his neck dropped him through a trapdoor. Bailey was the last person to be hanged for a crime in the United States.

In twentieth-century America, capital punishment across various states could be implemented by the electric chair, lethal injection, hanging, firing squad and the gas chamber. In twenty-first-century America, all of these methods are still legal, albeit in a dwindling number of states. The last occurrence of death by gas was in Arizona in 1999 and by firing squad in Utah in 2010. At the time of writing, the last death carried out by the electric chair was that of Nicholas Sutton, who opted for electrocution over lethal injection on February 20, 2020, at Riverbend Maximum Security Institution in Nashville, Tennessee. Following a seventeen-year hiatus from federal executions, on January 16, 2021, Dustin Higgs became the last and thirteenth person in a row to be executed (by lethal injection) by the federal government in the final month of Donald Trump's presidency.

All fifty states and U.S. territories are subject to the federal death penalty. In 2007, Ronell Wilson, a gang member of Staten Island's Stapleton Crew who murdered two undercover detectives in 2003 (and gained further press attention in 2013 for conducting a sexual relationship with and fathering the child of a Metropolitan Detention Center prison guard), became the first person to be federally sentenced to death in New York for more than half a century. The decision to execute Wilson was rescinded in 2016 due to a diagnosis of mental illness, making him ineligible for the death penalty under the Eighth Amendment. In 2019, the Supreme Court rejected the petition of convicted murderer Russell Bucklew in Missouri, who claimed that death by lethal injection would cause him great pain due to a preexisting condition. Associate Justice Neil Gorsuch argued that the Constitution's Eighth Amendment, which forbids cruel and unusual punishment, does not promise "a painless death."

According to data compiled by Austin Sarat, professor of jurisprudence and political science at Amherst College, in his book *Gruesome Spectacles: Botched Executions and America's Death Penalty* (based on the ESPY File execution database and the Washington, D.C. nonprofit Death Penalty Information Center), of the 8,776 executions carried out in the United States between 1900 and 2010, 276 (3.15 percent) were botched, with lethal injection topping the list.

Similar to the Edison/Westinghouse efforts to dissociate their wares from the act of execution, the American Medical Association does not want to be associated with it either. Over the years, for the same reason, certain pharmaceutical companies, conspicuous for their conscientiousness, have discontinued the anesthetic drugs used in lethal injection ingredients. Additionally, whereas veterinarian-administered animal euthanasia generally involves a two-injection method of sedation followed by induced cardiopulmonary arrest, many of the U.S. states where lethal injection is legal use a three-injection method. The third drug is a paralytic, and so if the recipient is in pain or distress, their paralysis prevents any clear observation of this. The lack of medical and pharmaceutical expertise has made lethal injection more of a trial-and-error practice and ultimately more of a failure than its predecessors.

New York State ended the death penalty in 1984, but in 1995, the newly elected governor of New York, George Pataki, reinstated it by means of lethal injection. In 2004, responding to the case of the *People v. LaValle* in which convicted murderer and rapist Stephen LaValle argued that his death sentence had been erroneously imposed due to unfair testimony and a biased juror, the New York Court of Appeals declared the death penalty statute unconstitutional. In 2007, the death penalty was formally abolished in New York and the last death sentence reduced to life. Up until the final death penalty execution of Eddie Lee Mays in 1963, New York State had the second-highest national execution rate after Virginia.

The flipside to the subject of capital punishment is the much-debated topic of assisted suicide, or medical aid in dying, that facilitates a person's wishes to end their suffering from a terminal or debilitating illness with the help of another person, more commonly a physician. It is distinct from euthanasia, which is defined by the *other* person being responsible for—rather than assisting with—the death of the person who requests it.

In the state of New York, patients have the right to refuse lifesaving medication. In 1997, a group of physicians and terminally ill patients led by Dr. Timothy E. Quill challenged the ban on physician-assisted suicide. New York attorney general Dennis Vacco argued the landmark *Vacco v. Quill* case before the Supreme Court and successfully defended New York State's prohibition on assisted suicide. Dr. Quill is a board member of the Death with Dignity National Center in Portland, Oregon, where the Death with Dignity Act was approved in the 1994 general election.

All fifty U.S. states and the federal government prohibit euthanasia under general homicide laws. However, the federal government has no assisted suicide laws, and it is now legal in more than half a dozen states. As per its position on capital punishment, the American Medical Association is opposed to physician-assisted suicide. The official standing is that it is unethical and in direct conflict with the Hippocratic Oath. Individual physicians who assist with suicide remain unlisted for reasons of confidentiality and their own safety. In the majority of cases, the method of death is an oral dosage of a barbiturate. Compared with intravenous drugs, death by oral dosage can take many hours, but the design is such that the recipient loses consciousness long before their body fades away.

On February 13, 2015, the Death with Dignity Act was introduced to the state of New York by Senators Brad Hoylman and Diane Savino. If passed, it would allow an individual with a terminal illness to request aid-in-dying medication, the right to rescind the request, the right to attain a physician and a death certificate and the right to construct a will and applicable insurance within the state of New York. On February 1, 2021, New York Assembly member Amy Paulin introduced the Medical Aid in Dying Act in a continuation of previous efforts. At the time of writing, the bill has been referred to the Assembly Health Committee.

Inquests for homicides, suicides, accidental and suspicious deaths are conducted by the Office of Chief Medical Examiner, which sits beside the cluster of hospitals, Hospital Row, on the eastern edges of Manhattan's Kips Bay and Murray Hill. Bellevue Hospital complex is the home of the New York City Mortuary, a constant since Bellevue's development of the city's first official morgue. Over fifty thousand people die in New York City each year. Of those, approximately five thousand are autopsied. Examinations also take place in the Forensic Pathology Centers of Brooklyn and Queens, while death certificates are issued by the New York City Department of Health and Mental Hygiene.

Article 20 of the "Articles of Eyre" (an eyre was a judicial circuit) formally established the office of coroner in England in 1194. To "keep the pleas of the Crown" is where *coroner*—from the Latin *corona*, meaning "crown"—originates. The coroner investigated and recorded anything that involved the king's assets with the aim of collecting pocket money for the king and his Crusades, or any of the procession of wars that Norman England vigorously participated in and profited from. A *murdrum*, from which the word *murder* is derived, was the fine charged to any town or village on which a Norman homicide happened to land. The assets of individuals lost to suspicious deaths, accidents or suicides could be gathered up and put in the Crown's coffers via the route of divine retribution.

The coroners of New York were often elected for their ability to turn a blind eye. More than one was caught in the act of billing the city for inquests that had never taken place by recycling old names on death registers. As medical know-how was not a requirement, the fact that only some coroners were physicians was incidental. Others were undertakers, politicians, salesmen and plumbers and one even a musician. From 1873 to 1876, Irish-born Richard Croker held the position. "Boss Croker," as he was known due to his running of the notoriously corrupt Democratic "machine" of New York, Tammany Hall, had clocked up quite the résumé as a gang leader, boxer and extortionist. In 1874, one year after becoming the city's coroner, Croker was accused of killing a political rival in a shooting incident during a brawl on Thirty-Fourth Street and Second Avenue. An undecided jury ultimately let him go. One of Croker's reports from the Coroner's Office in 1875 is indicative of the often-vague summary of death prior to the expansion of forensic evidence and criminal investigation: "Compression of the brain due to injury of the head received at the hands of some person or persons unknown to us."

New York Coroner's Report, 1875. *Courtesy of New York City Municipal Archive.*

More than a century earlier in 1749, the seemingly unambiguous death of Cornelius Quick, possibly in cahoots with his own name, probably took less time to occur than New York coroner John Burnet's verbose description:

The jurors upon their oaths do say that the said Cornelius Quick on the eighth day of this present month of August in the night of the same day being intoxicated in liquor fell asleep near a door in the garret in the house of Jacob Riker which opens into an alley belonging to the said house and fell down into the said alley and soon after by the fall aforesaid dyed.

The equally booze-laced death of mariner John Brady, assessed by the same coroner in June 1758, took considerably longer:

The jurors upon their oaths do say that the said John Brady on the ninth day of the aforesaid month of June about eleven a clock in the evening of the same day being very much intoxicated with strong liquors and attempting to make water out of a window in the house of Catherine Salter in the East Ward of the said City fell into the street and languished till about two a clock and then died.

In 1852, the number of Manhattan coroners doubled from two to four. Within a couple of years of the 1898 consolidation of the five boroughs into New York City, the Bronx, Staten Island, Brooklyn and Queens gained two coroners each. In 1915, the coroner of New York City position was abolished and replaced in 1918 with the Office of Chief Medical Examiner of the City of New York. From here on in, the chief medical examiner was tasked with investigating and identifying the manner and cause of murders, suicides and suspicious death, this time with all the necessary training and qualifications of a physician. The power to hold inquests now belonged to the district attorney.

Charles Norris, the director of laboratories at Bellevue Hospital and the first appointed chief medical examiner of New York, threw his own money into expanding and stocking his Bellevue laboratory for the groundbreaking toxicology experiments that would take place therein. He hired chemist Alexander Gettler, who had immigrated to New York as a child from the Austro-Hungarian Empire, and together they became pioneers of forensic criminal investigation. Gettler's reputation would secure his position as the father of American forensic toxicology, while Norris successfully held his chief medical examiner post from 1918 until his death in 1935.

On the morning of August 10, 2019, financier and sex offender Jeffrey Epstein was found hanged in his jail cell at the Metropolitan Correctional Center (MCC) in Lower Manhattan's Civic Center. Soon after, he was pronounced dead at the New York Presbyterian Hospital. Numerous well-known individuals have found themselves incarcerated inside the Brutalist architecture of MCC, in operation since 1975, including Gambino crime

Alexander Gettler and Charles Norris. *Public domain.*

family boss John Gotti, Ponzi scheme fraudster Bernie Madoff, Mexican drug lord Joaquin Guzmán ("El Chapo") and 2016 Trump campaign chairman and chief strategist Paul Manafort. Epstein's autopsy was conducted by Chief Medical Examiner Barbara Sampson, who ruled the death a suicide. Epstein's lawyers disputed the ruling. His death was the first recorded suicide at the MCC since 2006. Epstein's body should have been photographed as it was found, which it was not, and therefore the removal of his body from his cell violated the Bureau of Prisons protocol. Because of his death, all criminal charges against him were dismissed on August 29, 2019.

Michael Baden, a physician and pathologist, a forensic thriller novelist and the host of HBO's *Autopsy*, was New York's chief medical examiner from 1978 to 1979. Mayor Ed Koch removed Baden from his position following complaints about his conduct and record keeping from the New York district attorney and the health commissioner. Baden then took the same position in Suffolk County in Long Island but was dismissed for allegedly making comments about how to commit murder with undetectable poison. Baden's dismissal was later rescinded, but he chose to leave anyway. Since then, he has testified as an expert witness on behalf of a number of high-profile defendants, including O.J. Simpson and Phil Spector, in much-publicized criminal investigations. In October 2019, after Epstein's brother hired Baden to observe the autopsy, Baden announced that he disagreed with Sampson's suicide conclusion, stating that Epstein's neck injuries pointed to "homicide rather than suicide."

Baden's chief medical examiner successor was Elliot Gross in 1979. In 1987, Gross was dismissed, again by Mayor Ed Koch, due to accusations of producing misleading autopsy reports and trial testimonies relating to deaths in police custody and in police altercations. Gross's replacement, Charles Hirsch, is the namesake for the Charles S. Hirsch Center for Forensic Sciences, the forensic biology department of the Office of Chief Medical Examiner, which has the largest public DNA crime laboratory in North America. Hirsch oversaw the identification of victims from the September 11 World Trade Center attacks in 2001. Since 2007, the center has been responsible for the identification of the 21,905 human samples recovered from the site. In the aftermath of 9/11, the Office of Chief Medical Examiner developed the Unified Victim Identification System, a database system designed to handle critical fatality management functions in the event of another major catastrophe. This was a step up from DMORT, the Disaster Mortuary Operational Response Team, which consists of nationwide regional experts dedicated to identifying victims in the event of large-scale disasters. In the days after the Twin Tower attacks, 2,753 people were reported missing. Over 1,100 people, approximately 40 percent of those reported missing, have yet to be identified.

When thirty-four-year-old NYPD detective James Zadroga, who had spent many days assisting Manhattan's 9/11 rescue mission, died from respiratory disease in 2006, a New Jersey autopsy reported that his death

The 9/11 Memorial South Pool, where the South Tower once stood.

was a direct result of the Ground Zero toxicity. The report conflicted with a further autopsy presided over by New York's then chief medical examiner, Charles Hirsch. The Hirsch report claimed that Zadroga's cause of death was due to self-injected prescription drugs. Since the latter report received heavy criticism, a third opinion, which also contradicted Hirsch's findings, was provided by none other than Michael Baden.

On May 10, 2014, the remains of the unidentified World Trade Center victims were removed from the Office of Chief Medical Examiner and placed in a repository seventy feet below ground within the structure of the National September 11 Memorial & Museum complex. Some of the victims' family members wore black gags at the relocation ceremony in an act of protest. The gags represented their lack of say on the matter and the moving of the remains to a tourist attraction. Managed solely by the Office of Chief Medical Examiner, the repository includes a private reflection room for family members. The museum has a unique position regarding the definition of a cemetery. The repository, pinpointed by a plaque visible to museum visitors, is a temporary storage space for the unidentified until they can be identified and claimed. It also includes identified remains that some families have chosen not to inter elsewhere.

8

REMNANTS OF ISRAEL

On December 6, 1496, as a prerequisite of his marriage to Isabella of Aragon, King Manuel I of Portugal signed a decree to forcibly convert all Jews to Catholicism or otherwise be expelled. A decade later, the *conversos* fled the added indignity of the anti-Semitic Lisbon Massacre. Of those who fled to Holland, some moved on again during the seventeenth century to the Dutch-ruled New Holland capital of Recife in Brazil. When the territory was conquered by the Portuguese, their Inquisition zoned in on practicing Jews and the conversos, the latter of whom they accused of secretly practicing Judaism. Stuck in a rut between a religious paradox and New World conflict, twenty-three Sephardic Spanish and Portuguese Jews left Recife within the ordered ninety days and, after a series of misadventures, arrived in New Amsterdam in September 1654.

First impressions of the Dutch colony may have been that it was decidedly more tolerant than "Peg-Leg Pete," as its one-legged Director-General Peter Stuyvesant was nicknamed, presumably when he was out of earshot. An outspoken anti-Semite and a dogmatic Calvinist, Stuyvesant penned his opposition to the Jewish presence within his colony to his superiors in Holland, but the profit-focused resolve of the Dutch West India Company had little to do with religious bigotry or tolerance, as indicated in correspondence with Stuyvesant and the New Amsterdam burgomasters: "Your Honors should also please consider that many of the Jewish nation are principal shareholders in the Company."

In July 1655, the diminutive Jewish community of New Amsterdam petitioned the director-general "to be permitted to purchase a burying place for their nation," separate from the city's Christian catch-all cemetery. In February 1656, permission was granted for "a little hook of land situate[d] outside of this city for a burial place." Though the exact whereabouts of the Beth Haim (Hebrew word for graveyard meaning "House of Life") are unknown, its description has a lot in common with New York's second Jewish cemetery, an elevated patch of land much smaller than its original size in today's Two Bridges area of Lower Manhattan. The oldest existing Jewish cemetery in the United States as well as the second Jewish burial ground in Manhattan, the First Shearith Israel Graveyard, also known as the Chatham Square Cemetery, was founded in 1682 by Jewish merchant Joseph Bueno de Mesquita. The oldest grave with its headstone still intact belongs to one of his own kin, Benjamin Bueno de Mesquita, who died in 1683.

A letter written to the Classis of Amsterdam in March 1655 by Reverend Johannes Megapolensis, chief minister of New Amsterdam's Dutch Reformed Church and author of *A Short Account of the Mohawk Indians*, demonstrates the full bile of anti-Semitism, as well as the mixed bag of New Netherland colonists, whose collective faiths were evidently too overwhelming for the pastor:

> *These people have no other God than the unrighteous Mammon, and no other aim than to get possession of Christian property, and to win all other merchants by drawing all trade towards themselves. Therefore, we request your Reverences to obtain from the Lords Directors that these godless rascals, who are of no benefit to the country, but look at everything for their own profit, may be sent away from here. For, as we have here Papists, Mennonites and Lutherans among the Dutch; also many Puritans or Independents, and many Atheists and various other servants of Baal among the English under this Government, who conceal themselves under the name of Christians; it would create a still greater confusion, if the obstinate and immovable Jews came to settle here.*

Congregation Shearith Israel, established with the arrival of the Sephardic Jews in 1654, is the oldest Jewish congregation in the United States and was the only one in New York until the formation of B'nai Jeshurun in 1825. Shearith Israel had its first official synagogue built at Mill Street (now South William Street) in 1730. At a strategic military point overlooking the East River, the Shearith Israel Graveyard was used by the Patriots and then the

British during their occupation of Revolution-era New York. Within a year of the war's end on April 6, 1784, the New York legislature passed the Act of Religious Incorporation that enabled the official purchase of places of worship irrespective of religious practices.

Until the nineteenth century, the opportunity to convert Christian spouses to Judaism was either hard to come by or resistant. Shearith Israel outlawed intermarriage for the bulk of the eighteenth century. Consequently, members of the Jewish congregation who married outside of it were often lost to the Christian faith and Christian churchyard burial. The few who were permitted Jewish burial rites were banished to the outskirts of the Jewish burial ground.

In 1798, at the same time as the larger part of Congregation Israel was fleeing the yellow fever–gripped city, Columbia College student Walter Jonas Judah, an apprentice to Dr. David Hosack and one of the first Jews to attend medical school in New York, stayed behind to attend to the sick. Twenty-year-old Judah died from the disease that same year and was interred at the Shearith burial ground. In October 1999, Mayor Rudy Giuliani signed a bill to name the section of St. James Place that runs alongside the cemetery Walter Jonas Judah Street.

In spite of the 1823 ban on burials below Canal Street, interments took place at the first Shearith cemetery until 1833. For those who could afford it, the desire to be buried with kin was worth the city's hefty "penalty of two hundred and fifty dollars for every such offence." The Second Cemetery of Congregation Shearith Israel, initially an out-of-the-way burial place for Jewish epidemic victims, suicides and indigents, exists today as a tiny portion of its former self in a closeted corner of Greenwich Village. By 1829, the city's growth led to the Third Cemetery of the Spanish-Portuguese Synagogue in Chelsea. It remained in use until 1851, when the city prohibited burials south of Eighty-Sixth Street.

The series of prohibitions on New York City burial space during the nineteenth century paved the way for the 1847 Rural Cemetery Act, which allowed commercial burial grounds to operate beyond the church and synagogue in the rural acres of New York State. The biggest boom of commercial burial grounds sprung up along the borders of Kings and Queens Counties on Long Island in the present-day boroughs of Brooklyn and Queens. The maximum 250 acres per county of cemetery land that the act permitted created a scrum for the county borders. The Cemetery Belt, as it came to be known, a conglomerate of secular and multiple-faith burial grounds, includes reinterments from short-lived or reduced graveyards that were either sold or severely compromised by urban expansion. Jewish

The Third Cemetery of the Spanish Portuguese Synagogue in Flatiron District, Manhattan.

transfers were executed inside the careful exceptions to Jewish rules that would otherwise prohibit disinterment in order not to disturb the dead.

The Cemetery Belt's twelve-acre Beth Olam Cemetery, founded in 1851, represents the Russian doll backstory of the three Manhattan congregations who share it. In 1825, a group of central European members of the Shearith Israel congregation left to form their own Ashkenazic congregation, B'nai Jeshurun, the first of its kind in New York and the second Jewish congregation in New York. Like a lot of New York cemetery land, the site of the original Thirty-Second Street graveyard, from which the burials were reinterred at Beth Olam, was sold by the trustees and now bears the weight of Midtown Manhattan's Hotel Pennsylvania. Due to infighting within B'nai Jeshurun, a group broke off and formed their own Orthodox Temple Shaaray Tefila in the mid-1840s. Fifty years later, Shaaray Tefila became a Reform congregation. Beth Olam's red brick Metaher House, built to accommodate small funeral services and *tahara*—the cleansing of the deceased—may be the only religious building designed by Central and Prospect Parks codesigner Calvert Vaux. "The New Colossus" ("Give me your tired, your poor / Your huddled masses yearning to breathe free / The wretched refuse of your teeming shore."), written by Beth Olam resident Emma Lazarus in 1883 and inscribed on the pedestal of the Statue of Liberty, was for many years the sonnet welcoming the arrival of countless immigrant ships.

Until the mid-nineteenth century, New York's synagogue elders wielded immense control over Jewish religious life with a stronghold over the way in which people were buried. A chronological burial pattern was considered to be an equalizer that fastened the communal connection through a timeline of sequential death. The centuries-old tradition of burial societies—*Chevrot Kadisha*—who often clashed with the synagogue elders due to their influence as death-care organizers, were responsible for every aspect of preparation between death and burial, including guideline provisions on ritual mourning. Philanthropic mutual aid societies called *landsmanshaftn*, regularly unaffiliated with any New York synagogue and formed according to the shtetl or sect with which immigrants identified, were adept at fundraising for widows and children and providing assistance for Jewish immigrants seeking work and accommodation. The nonprofit organization Der Arbeter Ring (the Workmen's Circle, now the Workers' Circle) began in New York at the turn of the twentieth century as a mutual aid organization that assisted immigrants with life insurance, political action, social networking and burial plans. The older Jewish cemeteries of New York are often segmented into fraternal societies, to which membership benefited end-of-life planning as well as burial costs for unmarried individuals.

Temple Emanu-El, the first Reform Jewish congregation in New York, was founded in 1845 by German Jewish immigrants. Six years later, Temple Emanu-El's new cemetery, Salem Fields, constructed at the Kings/Queens Counties border, became the first Jewish rural cemetery and the first to sell plots to individual families and burial societies, thus freeing individuals from the sequential burial rules of the first Manhattan synagogues.

A sequence not of chronological death, but of achievement, is on proud display at the Cemetery Belt's Mount Carmel, where celebrated Yiddish writer Sholem Aleichem, whose short stories in *Tevye and His Daughters* (or *Tevye the Dairyman*) inspired the musical *Fiddler on the Roof*, is interred in Honor Row among a lineup of celebrated anarchists, writers, socialists and labor leaders. Across the road, a muddle of undefined boundaries with minimal signage confuses matters further with the names of the cemeteries therein: Union Field, New Union Field (also known as Beth El), Hungarian Union Field and the outlander in name only, Machpelah.

Union Field Cemetery, founded in 1878 by Congregation Rodeph Sholom after its Park Avenue burial ground had become exhausted, has at least two noteworthy interments who are inextricably linked with seminal fiction: Roy Cohn, who was Joseph McCarthy's chief counsel during the Red Scare and an advisor to a young Donald Trump, was also a central

Grave of Bert Lahr at Union Field Cemetery in Queens.

character in Tony Kushner's Pulitzer Prize–winning play *Angels in America*; and Bert Lahr, whose small flat grave marker would be easily missed if it wasn't for the regular clutter of tiny toy lions deposited there by fans of his Cowardly Lion portrayal in the 1939 movie *The Wizard of Oz*. The mausoleum of Joe Weber of Weber and Fields occupies Hungarian Union Field Cemetery. The success of the once popular double act, who had their own Broadway music hall, declined with the rise of the twentieth century. Their failure to hold the attention of Radio City Music Hall's audience at the venue's opening night in December 1932 was a key factor in them never appearing at a theater together ever again.

The six-acre Machpelah Cemetery, filled to capacity long ago, receives curious visitors for its most iconic resident, Hungarian American illusionist Harry Houdini. His Midtown Manhattan funeral at the New York Elks Lodge, at which he had been a member, drew around two thousand attendees. Houdini died at the age of fifty-two on Halloween in 1926 from peritonitis. Nine days prior to his death, the unprepared Houdini received a series of punches to the stomach from McGill University student Jocelyn Gordon Whitehead in Montreal, who wanted to test Houdini's claims of physical endurance. Based on the assumption that the blows contributed to Houdini's death, Whitehead signed the affidavit that enabled Houdini's wife and stage assistant Bess to collect her double indemnity claim from New York Life Insurance.

Grave of Harry Houdini at Machpelah Cemetery in Queens.

Crowning Houdini's impressive family plot is the crest of the Society of American Magicians, who initially took responsibility for the upkeep of his burial site since a series of Houdini busts were either stolen or destroyed. Plot sharer Theo Hardeen, another escape artist and magician, capitalized on his famous sibling by using the tagline "Brother of Houdini." Bess Houdini, who died almost twenty years after her husband, Harry, and whose Roman Catholic family wouldn't allow her to be buried in a Jewish burial ground, is interred twenty-plus miles north of the Bronx in Westchester's Gate of Heaven Cemetery.

The funeral arrangements of Eileen McKenney, the inspiration for the memoir *My Sister Eileen*, written by her sister Ruth McKenney, and the musical of the same name, took a different course. On December 22, 1940, Eileen's husband, *The Day of the Locust* and *Miss Lonelyhearts* author Nathanael West, a notoriously bad driver and presumably upset over the death of his friend F. Scott Fitzgerald the day before, ran a light into a fatal collision. Unlike her husband, who was also killed in the accident, McKenney wasn't Jewish. Although her ashes were added to her husband's grave at Mount Zion in Maspeth, Queens, her presence is elusive. West's brief epitaph reads simply: "Husband of Eileen."

Two halves of two double acts reside at Mount Zion: Lorenz Hart, the lyricist for the songwriting duo Rogers and Hart, and Isador "Izzy" Einstein of the Prohibition Bureau partnership Izzy and Moe (Smith).

During Prohibition, countless bartenders and bootleggers had Izzy and Moe to blame for their stints in jail. Their modus operandi involved multiple disguises that included Mexican laborers, Chinese launderers, African Americans in Harlem, rabbis and gravediggers. Izzy and Moe confiscated an estimated $15 million worth of booze and broke a record with seventy-one raids all in a night's work. Their adventures are detailed in Izzy's best-selling 1932 autobiography, *Prohibition Agent No. 1*, which he dedicated "to the 4,932 persons I arrested, hoping they bear me no grudge for having done my duty."

Further along in law enforcement, the Shomrim Society (from *Shomer*, meaning "guardian" or "watchman"), a fraternity of Jewish NYPD officers who established themselves during Prohibition in 1924, have a plot and memorial obelisk at Montefiore Cemetery in Springfield Gardens, Queens. Their society is different to the Orthodox neighborhood watch Shomrim who patrol Jewish neighborhoods as civilian volunteers and furthermore from the traditional Shomrim who watch over the dead until they are buried.

On the flipside of policing, a game of Jewish gangland connect the dots can be played with selected Queens cemeteries. After making enemies out of garment industry labor racketeer rivals, the young lives of the organized crime gang leaders the Shapiro brothers were surrendered to what was colloquially known in the criminal underworld as the "Chicago Overcoat." Irving and Meyer were killed by gunfire in 1931 when they were twenty-

Izzy and Moe.
Public domain.

seven and twenty-three, respectively. Three years later, at age twenty-three, their brother Willie was buried alive by organized hit squad Murder Inc. All three are interred at Mount Lebanon in Glendale. Meanwhile, two members of Murder Inc., Louis "Lepke" Buchalter and Emanuel "Mendy" Weiss, who were executed in Sing Sing's electric chair in 1944, are buried at Mount Hebron Cemetery in Flushing, as is fellow racketeer and extortionist Nathan "Kid Dropper" Caplin, who was executed outside Manhattan's Lower East Side New Essex Market Courthouse on the orders of labor slugger and bootlegger Jacob "Little Augie" Orgen in 1923. Little Augie got his comeuppance four years later when he was killed in a drive-by shooting by Louis Lepke and fellow Murder Inc. cohort Jacob "Gurrah" Shapiro (buried at Queens' Montefiore Cemetery). Orgen's headstone at Mount Judah Cemetery in Ridgewood is engraved with a deliberate error; his age when he died was thirty-four and not twenty-six as it is written. When Orgen put together his "Little Augies" gang at the age of twenty-six, his Austrian Orthodox Jewish father decided to stop the clock on his son's activities by disowning his advancing criminal years. Little Augie's intentionally inaccurate grave marker is the ultimate parental final word.

Orthodox burial tradition has an egalitarian arrangement with one person per grave. Many of the groups belonging to Orthodox Judaism allow mausoleums if the deceased are buried beneath the ground. Based on the historic rock-cut tombs of Jerusalem such as the Tombs of Absalom and Benei Hezir, Reform Judaism permits above-ground interment. The Sanctuary mausoleum at Mount Lebanon Cemetery in Queens was the first indoor community mausoleum in New York City. In the traditional Jewish faith, the body is regarded as a vessel on loan from God. While embalming and cremation are strictly forbidden by Orthodox Judaism, some Reform Jews have incorporated them into their funeral arrangements.

The Kohanim Hands, depicting the priestly blessing of the *Kohen* or *Cohen*—"priest" in Hebrew—are a frequent feature of Jewish cemeteries. Those whose names are variations of Kohen, such as Coen, Caan, Khan and Kohn, are considered by some to have patrilineal ancestry in the Kohanim, the priests of the Temple of Jerusalem, who are believed to be the direct male descendants of Aaron, the brother of Moses. The hands nevertheless appear on grave markers with many different names. Kohanim are forbidden from being in direct contact with the dead so as not to become impure (*tamei*), another tradition that goes back to the Temple of Jerusalem. This is the reason why, unless the space of a town or city is compromised, synagogues and burial grounds are geographically separate. In New York

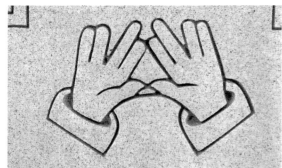

Left: Enamel grave photo.

Above: Kohanim Hands.

City, the rule is complemented by the remoteness of the Cemetery Belt. With a gap midway between the fingers, the Kohanim Hands are a familiar image to *Star Trek* fans. Leonard Nimoy's decision to adopt the hand sign for his character Spock's "live long and prosper" Vulcan salute was inspired by the blessings he had witnessed at temple as a boy.

Memorial portraiture, popular in the late nineteenth and early twentieth centuries with Italians and eastern European Jewish immigrants, is another common feature of New York's older cemeteries. The effect was achieved by burning photographic images onto enamel plates. The Talmud has a very literal position regarding the Second Commandment, "Thou shalt not make unto thee any graven images," and prohibits human likenesses on graves. Be that as it may, enameling and modern laser-etching have loosened the rules for non-Orthodox Jews. Photo-realistic laser-etched portraits of the deceased on black shiny headstones are popular with Soviet and post–Soviet era Jews, who became more secular during and after the reign of Communism. The lasered graves cut striking lines through the jam-packed Washington Cemetery in Mapleton, Brooklyn. In sharp contrast to the older weathered gray or tree stump graves, they have seized peripheries, paths and corners. At Washington Cemetery, the contentious issue of cemetery space is pressing, quite literally, against an overflow of hopscotch headstones.

There are just over a million Jews living in New York City, roughly 13 percent of the city's population and the highest density of Jewish people in any city in the world outside of Tel Aviv. European pogroms pushed mass Jewish

Washington Cemetery in Brooklyn.

migration to America from the 1880s until the quota-based Immigration Act of 1924. By the mid-twentieth century, dozens of synagogues in the Lower East Side had dissolved or spread out as new generations of Jewish Americans handled their own independence or moved away from New York into new communities with new synagogues. Many of the old landsmanshaftn, fraternities and lodges that had banded together to provide practical and cultural guidance disappeared. Distant heirs and waning societies were left with the nagging problem of timeworn burial plots.

Negotiable black market plot sales conducted between a financially burdened society and a nonmember beneficiary can and do occur. Selling plots for cash at not-for-profit cemeteries has its limitations inasmuch as they can only be sold back to the cemetery at the original cost with 4 percent simple interest per year. As unprofitable as this is, in New York State the cemetery has the right of first refusal. If the cemetery turns down the sale, then the owner of the plot can sell beyond the cemetery. Regularly, multiple plots are traded wholesale. Therefore, the buyer may then violate New York's not-for-profit rules by relying on the cemetery to sell the individual plots on their behalf. In the meantime, burial fees paid to the cemetery keep the business solvent. On account of such complications, there have been occasions in which a person has visited the graveside of their relative or spouse only to find their reserved space occupied by an expired stranger.

Burial space, and indeed, gathering space, became a worldwide issue in 2020 with the onslaught of the COVID-19 pandemic. The Orthodox communities of Brooklyn's Borough Park and Williamsburg were hit especially hard by the virus. Many people within those communities felt that they were being harassed by the city with regards to the pandemic's social distancing rule that conflicted with a highly sociable way of life. A case in point is the public chastisement by Mayor Bill de Blasio and the law enforcement breakup of hundreds of Hasidic mourners at Rabbi Chaim Mertz's funeral gathering in Williamsburg in the spring of 2020. Beth Israel Cemetery in New Jersey, where many of Brooklyn's Hasidic Jews are buried, and Mount Richmond Cemetery in Staten Island provided urgent burial space during the 2020 coronavirus peak.

Mount Richmond, along with Silverlake Cemetery, also in Staten Island, is managed by the Hebrew Free Burial Association (HFBA). Having provided burials for over sixty-five thousand indigent Jews since its beginnings in the Lower East Side in the 1880s, HFBA is the largest society of its kind outside of Israel. According to David Oshinsky's book *Bellevue: Three Centuries of Medicine and Mayhem at America's Most Storied Hospital*, an attendant at Bellevue morgue once tricked the HFBA into burying the body of an unclaimed Irishman by placing a Jewish newspaper in his pocket.

In January 1960, the Protestant Episcopal bishop of New York, the Auxiliary Roman Catholic bishop of New York and the president of the American Jewish Congress gathered with hundreds of attendees at the Stephen Wise Free Synagogue on the Upper West Side to address the proficiency of state laws in preventing anti-Semitism. The catalyst was the nationwide anti-Semitic desecrations that included the smearing of eighty-seven headstones at Baron Hirsch Cemetery in Graniteville, Staten Island, with yellow painted swastikas and the word *fuhrer*. Bayside and the neighboring Acacia and Mokom Sholom Cemeteries in Brooklyn are among the few that have been desecrated to a level that surpasses disaffected delinquency. Late twentieth-century atrocities have included impaling and burning corpses and bowling with a skull torn from a skeleton. The Community Alliance for Jewish-affiliated Cemeteries, born out of an effort to repair and maintain the previously neglected Bayside Cemetery, is an organization that is dedicated to restoring, protecting and cataloguing the graves of Jewish cemeteries.

Manhattan's nondenominational Trinity Church Cemetery and Mausoleum sold one of its last remaining plots according to its policy of extraordinary circumstances. Ed Koch, perhaps because he was the mayor of New York City or because he was willing to pay $20,000 for a plot,

"Jewish Gate" for Mayor Koch at Trinity Church Cemetery and Mausoleum in Manhattan.

qualified for the extraordinary circumstances. Possibly in defense of the sum he paid for the plot five years prior to his death, Koch confessed, "The idea of leaving Manhattan permanently irritates me." A "Jewish Gate" sign was added to the eastside cemetery gate near the Koch plot at his behest. When Koch was buried in 2013, a mistake on his tombstone switched his birthdate from 1924 to 1942. His particulars, since corrected, are listed above the final words of the murdered journalist Daniel Pearl: "My father is Jewish, my mother is Jewish, I am Jewish."

9

THE LONESOME AND THE LEFTOVERS

Aquehonga Manacknong, believed to mean "the place of bad woods," was the Lenape name for Staten Island, the so-called forgotten borough. In many respects, Staten Island is the most interesting borough due to its striking difference from the other four, its urban reluctance and the palpable remains of its human history. At the geographical heart of Staten Island, amid an abundance of wildlife—white-tailed deer, garter snakes, wild turkeys, red and brown bats and snapping turtles—is the 1,778-acre Greenbelt, which is the second-largest parkland in all five boroughs after Pelham Bay Park in the Bronx. A dense forest of oak, beech, hickory and red maple trees, the parkland boasts the highest natural point in New York City and one of the highest on the Eastern Seaboard, Todt Hill, translated from Old High German as "Dead Hill." On the edge of the Greenbelt's Latourette Park and Blood Root Valley, in overgrown woods surrounded by an insecure wire fence and buffered by a fortress of lacerating thorns, is a place synonymous with urban legends, horror stories and institutional neglect. What remains of the New York Farm Colony is the beating heart of childhood nightmares and adolescent mischief.

The Richmond County Poor Farm, established in 1829 and renamed the New York Farm Colony after the 1898 consolidation of the five boroughs, functioned as a Department of Public Charities almshouse for the poor, the sick, the destitute, the mentally ill and the elderly. Able-bodied indigents worked on the farm in exchange for food and board. In 1915, the farm colony merged with the neighboring Seaview Hospital and grew

New York Farm Colony ruins in Staten Island.

to approximately 320 acres. At the farm's busiest, the number of inmates exceeded one thousand. One of its old-age residents, Alice Austen, was separated from her partner of more than fifty years and placed in the colony in 1950 by disapproving relatives. Her photographs of late nineteenth- and early twentieth-century New York, as well as intimate lesbian life on Staten Island, would make her a posthumous LGBTQ icon.

The colony waned with the advent of social security but lingered on until 1975, after which it became a playground for angry graffiti, loitering deer, urban explorers, shelter-seeking homeless, structural decline and real and imagined deviancy. The ruins of multiple dormitories, a dining hall, an insane pavilion and a morgue are awash with asbestos and partially collapsed ceilings and elevator shafts. In the New York Farm Colony, the dying season is ever-present and will remain so until new arrangements take effect.

In 2016, the New York City Economic Development Corporation's plan to sell forty-five acres of the derelict colony to a Staten Island developer for one dollar was approved by the City Council. The developer's plan was to invest in the building of affordable accommodation for senior citizens, thereby retaining some cultural continuity, while keeping some of the old buildings as attractive reinforced ruins. If that well-intentioned plan goes ahead, then the colony's potter's field, which no longer has headstones and sits under a tangle of red thorns, will presumably stay put and be memorialized. The New York Farm Colony cemetery was active for an unknown number of years, although records show that interments occurred in the early 1900s, with a rumored additional space for Seaview Hospital's amputated limbs.

Two other fading Staten Island cemeteries in similar prohibited overgrown areas contain thousands of burials from the Merchant Marine Hospital and the Sailors Snug Harbor Retirement Home. The remains of Captain Robert Richard Randall, whose death in 1801 put forth the will that made the retirement home possible, takes pride of place (since he was moved from Saint Mark's Church in-the-Bowery Churchyard) beneath a memorial obelisk in front of the former retirement complex, now the Snug Harbor Cultural Center & Botanical Garden.

Some of the older cemeteries on Staten Island have been partially brought back to life by the commendable efforts of FACSI (Friends of Abandoned Cemeteries of Staten Island), who, apart from restoring and maintaining forgotten or abandoned burial grounds, locate and log the records of the interred. One of the FACSI graveyards, the Methodist Asbury Cemetery—formerly New Springfield Cemetery—has a white obelisk grave that belongs to a certain Colonel Ichabod Crane. While serving as aide-de-camp to the governor of New York during the War of 1812, Washington Irving met Crane and penciled-in his memorable name for later use. Crane, who wasn't at all pleased with his namesake in Irving's short story "The Legend of Sleepy

Hollow," is buried with his wife, Charlotte; his son William; and "Juan," a Native American Umpqua boy from Oregon who Crane brought to his household in Staten Island to work as a servant. Prior to becoming surgeon general of the army, Crane's second son, Charles Henry Crane, who is buried at Arlington National Cemetery in Virginia, was an attending doctor at the deathbed of President Lincoln.

Graniteville's Hillside Cemetery, also a FACSI burial ground, is associated with a dark little tale due to the joint burial of Emeline Housman and her baby daughter Ann Eliza, whose bodies were found beaten and burned after a house fire on Christmas Day 1843. The suspect, Emeline's sister-in-law, Polly Bodine, dubbed "the witch of Staten Island" by P.T. Barnum's wax tableau of the crime scene, was acquitted after three trials. Almost two centuries later, Bodine continues

Grave of Ichabod Crane at Asbury Cemetery in Staten Island.

to be regarded as the likely culprit. Other FACSI affiliates include the tiny eighteenth-century burial grounds of prominent Staten Island families such as the Sylvan Grove Cemetery and the Sleight Family Graveyard, otherwise known as Blazing Star Cemetery, which lies adjacent to the Staten Island Boat Graveyard in the Arthur Kill.

Owing to the array of contagious diseases caught aboard the passenger ships to New York, the fate of many thousands of mostly Irish migrants was to perish in immigration quarantine and be buried in the mass graves of the Marine Hospital Quarantine Cemetery. An X marks the spot in the form of a commemorative FACSI signpost, fixed into the front lawn of the Richmond County Supreme Court above the immeasurable dead. During the Staten Island Quarantine War of 1858, a mob, resentful of the threat of yellow fever on their island, set fire to the multiple hospital buildings that constituted the quarantine, a marginally cordial event given that they removed the patients first. The *New York Times* reported, "These attentions to the helpless creatures were a redeeming feature."

Just off Staten Island's South Beach in the Lower New York Bay, the names of two artificial islands made from landfill, a mile apart and with less than fifteen acres between them, sound like a respectable law firm. Hoffman and Swinburne (John Hoffman was a New York mayor and governor and John Swinburne was mayor of Albany and Port of New York health officer) were constructed in response to the Staten Island Quarantine War and used as quarantine stations for thousands of symptomatic new arrivals. Through the 1920s, the Hoffman and Swinburne quarantine numbers dwindled due to clean water and vaccines. Today, the ruins on Swinburne Island include a conspicuous-looking chimney. In a photograph taken during the island's active quarantine years by Staten Island resident and fleeting farm colony resident Alice Austen, the chimney forms part of a crematorium, the last full-bodied stop for the unluckiest of migrants.

The 1.5-mile-long City Island in the Long Island Sound off the Bronx is a rarity among the small islands of New York City due to its human habitation. Many New Yorkers are oblivious to its existence. Its active waterside burial ground, Pelham Cemetery, was built to accommodate the island's nineteenth-century maritime community. Elsewhere in the Bronx borough, in Mott Haven, a crypt belonging to the Morris family (after whom *Morrisania* in the Bronx is named) at Saint Ann's Episcopal Church, is exclusive to its very own churchyard. The church was built in 1840 by New York and Harlem Railroad vice president Gouverneur Morris Jr. in honor of his mother, Ann Cary Randolph Morris, a direct descendent of

Left: Swinburne Island view photographed by Alice Austen. *Courtesy of Alice Austen House.*

Below: Pelham Cemetery on City Island, with a view of Hart Island in the background.

Pocahontas. His father, Gouverneur Morris Sr., who is also interred in the family crypt, was a founding father, "penman of the Constitution" and leader of the 1811 Commissioners Street Plan for New York City. The minutiae of the lead-up to Gouverneur Sr.'s death in 1816 was described in troubling detail by his friend, New York senator and signee of the Constitution Rufus King:

> *Mr. Gouverneur Morris was not expected to live thro' yesterday. He has been long subject to a stricture in the urinary Passage; and have unskillfully forced a piece of whale bone thro' the Canal so lacerated the parts, as to*

create a very high degree of inflammation, which has been followed by a
mortification that I am told will prove fatal. Some years ago, and in the
interior of our State, he performed the same operation with a flexible piece
of hickory; the success on this occasion probably emboldened him to repeat
the experiment, that is now to prove fatal.

There are six presidents buried in New York State (there would be seven had President James Monroe not been disinterred from Manhattan's New York City Marble Cemetery and reinterred at Hollywood Cemetery in Richmond, Virginia, in 1858). One-third of those six—both Roosevelts—and almost one-third (fourteen) of the forty-six U.S. presidents were Freemasons. The fraternity that emerged from the medieval stonemason guilds of Europe, who formed lodges with mystic and courtly rituals, grew progressively more secular during the Enlightenment. The Masonic symbol of the square and compass, the tools of the stonemason trade, often accompanied by a letter *G* that may represent either *geometry* or *God*, is commonplace among the cemeteries of America. Ulysses S. Grant, who was not a Freemason but did belong to that other ancient fraternity, the Odd Fellows, is the only president interred in New York City. The General Grant National Memorial, or Grant's Tomb, as it is commonly known, at Riverside Park in Morningside Heights, is North America's largest mausoleum with a 150-foot-high exterior.

The word *mausoleum* comes from the tomb of Mausolus, upon which Grant's Tomb is architecturally based. Mausolus ruled the First Persian Empire, and his grand burial tomb, constructed in the fourth century BCE in present-day Turkey and destroyed by a series of midmillennia earthquakes, was one of the Seven Wonders of the Ancient World. President Grant, previously the commanding general of the Union army, died in 1885, a year after losing his life savings to a pyramid scheme. His remains were transferred to his mausoleum from a nearby temporary burial space on April 17, 1897, twelve years after his funeral had been attended by over one million people. As a result of the biggest public fundraising effort at that time, over $600,000 paid for the tomb's construction. Inside, the smooth red quartzite twin sarcophagi of Ulysses and his wife, Julia, who joined him in 1902, are based on Napoleon's tomb at Les Invalides in Paris. A familiar decorative and often empty funerary vessel in the grander cemeteries of New York, the sarcophagus combines the Greek words *sarco* (flesh) and *phagus* (to eat) and harks back to the writings of Roman philosopher Pliny the Elder, who confidently believed that the limestone

Grant's Tomb in Manhattan.

used in the common sarcophagus accelerated decomposition: "It is a well-known fact, that dead bodies, when buried in this stone, are consumed in the course of forty days, with the sole exception of the teeth."

The construction and whereabouts of Grant's Tomb drew the attention of New Yorkers toward a much-smaller grave, situated a short two-minute walk north of the mausoleum. A small plinth with a granite urn on top, called the Amiable Child Monument, marks the grave of a five-year-old boy named Saint Claire Pollack, who died on July 15, 1797. No one knows exactly how his death occurred, but the most common assumptions bounce between a tumble at the nearby cliffs, a drowning accident or yellow fever. The contrasting graves of Grant and Pollack, together with the Flatiron District's Worth Monument (where General William Jenkins Worth, who fought in the 1812 and Mexican American Wars and after whom Fort Worth in Texas is named, is interred) are unique for their solitary Manhattan locations on city-owned land.

A Google Maps glance at Westchester County, just north of New York City, may draw the eye to a "points of interest" marker called Hermit's Grave in Irvington Woods, less than a ten-minute drive from the Sunnyside house that belonged to the area's namesake, author Washington Irving. The Hermit's Grave headstone was erected in memory of Johann Wilhelm Stolting, a German-born linguist teacher turned—as the Google Maps marker suggests—recluse, who lived alone in the woods and sold handmade wooden buttons. A resourceful chap, he made a coffin that doubled as his

Amiable Child Monument in Manhattan.

bed and was buried in it on his death in 1888. Stolting's grave bears the honorary distinction of being the only marked grave in the village of Irvington.

Ferncliff Cemetery in Hartsdale, also in Westchester, is a place where many former New York City residents dwell. The flat markers in its grounds are indistinct but for the identity of selected dead: Paul Robeson, James Baldwin and Malcolm X. Meanwhile, a procession of A-listers has gone the way of Ferncliff's crematory: John Lennon, Christopher Reeve, Nelson Rockefeller and Jim Henson. Chiefly, Ferncliff is a place of exclusive indoor interment with a lonesome ivory tower environment designed for those seeking an eternity in affluent seclusion. While particular rooms and alcoves have been customized by the family members of the deceased, the elder statesman Ferncliff Mausoleum, otherwise known as the Cathedral of Memories; the Shrine of Memories middle mausoleum; and the newer, brighter, shinier Rosewood Mausoleum, appear clinically detached like a polished Kubrickian morgue. An atmosphere of through-the-keyhole surveillance tracks its maze of endless corridors, indecipherable coordinates and stained-glass windows that cast tinted shadows instead of light. Of the three mausoleums, only Rosewood has regular available crypt space for noncremated remains, but as its website affirms: "Occasionally, Ferncliff Cemetery reacquires burial rites to property in the Shrine of Memories and Ferncliff Mausoleum."

To satisfy her West Coast descendants, in 2017, former Ferncliff resident Judy Garland was transferred almost fifty years after her death to Los Angeles's Hollywood Forever Cemetery. The L.A. cemetery has a memorial monument dedicated to Garland's canine costar from *The Wizard of Oz*, Toto (real name Terry), which is often mistaken for an actual grave. In fact, Toto's remains have lain under a section of California's Ventura Freeway ever since the ranch belonging to Hollywood dog trainer Carl Spitz was demolished to make room for Route 101. Back in Westchester, situated just two and a half miles away from Ferncliff Cemetery, Hartsdale Pet Cemetery, founded in 1896, claims to be the oldest continuously operating pet cemetery in the world.

Top: General William Jenkins Worth Monument in Manhattan.

Bottom: Rosewood Mausoleum at Ferncliff Cemetery in Westchester County, New York. *Author's photo with permission of Ferncliff Cemetery.*

Perhaps no other burial ground represents the city of New York like Cypress Hills Cemetery, established in 1848 as the first nonsectarian cemetery for Kings and Queens Counties. Its 225 acres in the rolling hills of Brooklyn and Queens are a candid representation of the migrant and the settler.

Years after immigrating to America, Ignacy Jan Paderewski, the world-renowned pianist and composer regularly mobbed by fans, former prime minister of the Republic of Poland and signee of the Treaty of Versailles, announced, "My heart belongs to America." Paderewski let it be known that in accordance with medieval European highborn tradition, he wished for his heart to be placed in the land that he loved and not returned to Nazi-occupied Poland. Upon Paderewski's death in Manhattan in 1941, his Polish-born friend John Smolenski, a New York State assemblyman, mortician and owner of the John Smolenski Funeral Home in Greenpoint, Brooklyn, prepared Paderewski's body for a state funeral and interment at Arlington National Cemetery in Virginia and dutifully took out his heart. When Smolenski died in 1953, the whereabouts of Paderewski's heart remained a mystery until it was spotted in 1958 in a labeled urn in Cypress Hills Abbey, a huge, imposing, civic-looking indoor community mausoleum at Cypress Hills Cemetery, one floor beneath Mae West and "Gentleman Jim" Corbett. In 1992, after the fall of the Soviet Union, the heartless remains of Paderewski were transferred from Virginia to Saint John's Archcathedral in Warsaw, Poland. Whatever is left of the heart of Paderewski, whose name has been adopted by two annual American music festivals, now resides inside a spreadeagle piano-keyed bronze sculpture in the Polish-American Roman Catholic National Shrine of Our Lady of Czestochowa near Doylestown,

Cypress Hills Abbey in Brooklyn.

Pennsylvania. The absence of the heart at its former dwelling at Cypress Hills is marked by a commemorative label that reads: "Ignacy Jan Paderewski 1860–1941. His Heart Rested Here 1945–1986."

A cenotaph is an empty tomb or monument for remains that are missing or interred elsewhere. The James Gamble Rogers–designed Egyptian mastaba–style Straus Mausoleum at Woodlawn Cemetery in the Bronx has a cenotaph in the shape of a galley ship at its gated border, dedicated to Macy's co-owner and New York congressman Isidor Straus and his wife, Ida. When Isador resisted escaping in the *Titanic* lifeboats in 1912 in order to let women and children go first, Ida refused to leave his side, and both of them perished aboard the sinking ship. Isador's remains, retrieved from the ocean

Straus family mausoleum
at Woodlawn Cemetery in
the Bronx. *Hermis Pena/The
Woodlawn Cemetery & Conservancy.*

and interred at New Union Field Cemetery, were later transferred to the Straus family mausoleum beside an urn filled with water from the wreck, a tribute to Ida, who was never found. Straus Park, with its bronze nymph centerpiece on the Upper West Side, is an additional memorial to the pair. In Battery Park, the Wireless Operators Memorial, dedicated in 1915, is a cenotaph that honors wire operators lost at sea, including Jack Phillips, who was the radio operator aboard the *Titanic*.

Relocating human remains in New York City has always been a complicated, messy and often negligent business and an obvious frustration to the New Yorkers who bury their loved ones, only to have them dug up again or paved over for the sake of urban growth. On April 4, 1911, the *New York Times* reported the following in relation to Trinity Church Cemetery and Mausoleum:

> *It was said yesterday that in several of these graves the coffins had apparently never been occupied. What had become of the bodies which had been destined to them, or why empty coffins had been buried, no one could say, but a representative of Trinity Corporation was asked about the report and confirmed it. He suggested as a possible explanation that when the bodies were removed forty-two years ago to permit of the extension of Broadway through the cemetery the workmen had been careless in the performance of their task, and in order to conceal the resultant confusion had buried empty coffins, so that the new graves might agree in number with the old.*

The construction of Manhattan's Lower East Side tenements uprooted a cluster of churches and their corresponding early nineteenth-century cemeteries in the area around Houston Street. In the mid-1800s, the burials from local churchyards, including the Presbyterian, Methodist and First Baptist Cemeteries, were reinterred elsewhere, mostly within the Cemetery Belt. Prior to the 2005 completion of Avalon Chrystie Place, now The Chrystie, a retail and rental apartment building on Houston Street, archaeological testing found bone fragments and nineteenth-century artifacts. These were the leftovers from the traditional Quaker unmarked graves that had somehow slipped the transfer to a rural area of Brooklyn by a toll road called the Coney Island Plank Road.

When the surrounding Brooklyn landscape was elegantly cultivated into Prospect Park in the 1860s by Central Park co-designers Frederick Law Olmsted and Calvert Vaux, the Friends Cemetery remained as a private property. It is easily missed by Prospect Park visitors and yet partially visible through its surrounding wire fence. Early Quakers shunned tombstones, and so the dead of almost two centuries, plus the older two-thousand-plus reinterments from Houston Street and further reinterments from Brooklyn's former Wallabout Cemetery quite possibly exceed three thousand. Among the buried is movie star Montgomery Clift, who died in 1966 at the age of forty-five in his Manhattan townhouse on the Upper East Side. Clift's cause of death, "occlusive coronary artery disease," was determined by the young associate medical examiner who performed the autopsy, Michael Baden, the future chief medical examiner of New York (before he was fired by Ed Koch) and the second opinion observer of Jeffrey Epstein's autopsy. Clift's qualifying status for interment at the Friends Cemetery was his practicing Quaker mother.

West of Houston Street, the Greenwich Village Society for Historic Preservation opposed the construction of a SoHo hotel even before the excavation of a parking lot uncovered human remains in 2006. The Dominick, a $450 million, 46-story, 391-unit hotel that changed its name from the Trump SoHo a year into Donald Trump's presidency, occupies the site of the former Spring Street Presbyterian Church. Incorporated in 1811 and demolished in 1966, the church, targeted in the Anti-Abolitionist Riots of 1834, had been among the few that had a mixed-race abolitionist congregation in the years before New York State outlawed slavery. Use of the Spring Street burial vaults occurred from the early 1820s until the mid-1840s. After the parking lot discovery, archaeologists identified four burial vaults containing the fragmented bones and intact burials of around two hundred adults and children. The Spring Street remains, sent to Syracuse University for analysis until 2013, were later reinterred at Brooklyn's Green-Wood Cemetery.

The former Saint John's Burying Ground in Greenwich Village, associated with Saint John's Chapel of Trinity Parish and active for the first half of the nineteenth century, is a short walk north of the Dominick. What could be described as the workman's burden happened again in 1939 when construction workers, hired to renovate a park, discovered a vault containing an Egyptian sarcophagus–style iron casket with a glass window in the lid, a design that could have been crafted by Fisk & Raymond. Inside were the remains of six-year-old Mary Elizabeth Tisdall, who, since her death in 1850, had remained impressively preserved down to her blonde hair and white silk dress. She was reinterred in the catacombs of Trinity Church.

It is estimated that 10,000 people were buried at Saint John's Burying Ground before it was reconfigured into Saint John's Park in the 1890s by Irish-born New York alderman and assemblyman William Henry Walker, who lived at nearby St. Luke's Place. The name of the park changed to Hudson Park and then again in 1947 to its current name, James J. Walker Park, after William's son, the corrupt yet goodtime mayor of Prohibition-era New York. Just prior to the park's construction, only around 250 bodies were dug up for reinterment elsewhere by the wealthier relatives of the dead. At the less fortunate end of circumstance, aside from the thousands of human remains left behind, is twenty-two-year-old prostitute Helen Jewett, whose brutal murder in 1836 launched a newspaper sensation as well as the beginnings of investigative journalism. Jewett's body was buried at Saint John's and—if the sensationalist *New York Herald* is to be believed—snatched for dissection soon after. In the present-day James J. Walker Park, a monument, erected for two firefighters who died in 1834 while on duty, is the last visible remnant of the cemetery.

The Queens-based playgrounds of Wayanda (Queens Village Pauper Burial Ground), Martin's Field (The Olde Towne of Flushing Burial Ground—since memorialized with a commemorative tablet and signage) and Newtown (Old Newtown Cemetery and then potter's field), together with the parking lot behind Elmhurst's Old Saint James Episcopal Church, sit atop burial grounds that were either partially dug up and transferred to other cemeteries or simply shrugged off and paved over.

In 1794, the Common Council fashioned a new potter's field in today's Flatiron District. The restless burial ground was nevertheless short-lived and a less busy area to the south was selected as a replacement. Skulls and bones were unearthed from the former burial site by sewer excavators and plumbers more than once during the early twentieth century. By then, the land had been cultivated into Madison Square Park.

In 1797, a Greenwich Village residents' petition opposing the new potter's field, which included the signature of Alexander Hamilton, proved unsuccessful. That same burial ground, dug out of a haven for people escaping the epidemics of the city, was where the infected dead, along with the indigent dead, were deposited. Church burial plots, such as the one belonging to the African Methodist Episcopal Zion Church, added to the volume. The potter's field became a military parade ground in 1826, and in 1833, "the row"—a handsome chain of red brick Greek Revival townhouses—was erected overlooking the parade ground turned park. The New York City Parks Department remodeled the park in the 1870s, and in 1880, Henry James's novel *Washington Square* spread word of the vicinity far beyond New York City. Deep down below the 9.75 acres of Washington Square Park, and impervious to the square's historic rallying cries, seminal music and literary output, are the remains of an estimated twenty thousand people.

Washington Memorial Arch foundation diggers in 1890 and Con Edison workers in 1965 are just a couple of examples of the accidental death detectors of Washington Square Park. So far in the twenty-first century, archaeologists and the usual construction worker suspects have found dozens of human remains, including intact burials and occupied vaults. Recent intact burials discoveries were left untouched due to Landmarks Preservation Commission protocol, while bone fragments, gathered for study, were reinterred in March 2021 in a wooden box beneath an engraved paving stone.

Washington Square Park.

In the wake of the 1823 ban on burials beneath Canal Street, the Common Council proposed a new burial ground at Murray Hill, more than three miles from the city at what an irked *Evening Post* writer deemed a "remote and inconvenient distance from the main seat of its population." The selected area was first conceived as having vaults and a pleasing aesthetic. By 1826, the Common Council acknowledged that the Greenwich Village potter's field had become a "public burying ground on an extensive Scale." The new Murray Hill City Burying Ground, considered too "springy and wet" for burial after some revision, nevertheless functioned as a pass-the-pauper reinterment ground for at least a couple of years. When the plans for constructing Croton Distributing Reservoir went ahead at Murray Hill in the early 1840s, it can only be assumed that the New York habit of dragging the dead occurred yet again. The deep foundations of the Croton reservoir at Forty-Second Street and Fifth Avenue, together with the greater need to receive clean water for the city, are *almost* a guarantee that the removal of human remains was successful. At the turn of the twentieth century, the distributing reservoir site became the home of the present-day Main Branch of the New York Public Library.

The relocated Murray Hill dead would have traveled a little farther north to Fiftieth Street, where the new city burial ground was already thriving and where skeletons were regularly prodded and poked by morbidly playful New Yorkers. Numerous complaints emerged regarding the sight and smell of exposed coffins and human remains due to the widening of Fourth Avenue. In 1858, an estimated 100,000 burials were removed from the Fiftieth Street site—where the Waldorf-Astoria Hotel now stands—and transferred to Wards Island.

Between the upper east side of Manhattan and northwest Queens, Randall's Island Park is the collective name for three islands, Randall's and Wards Islands and Sunken Meadow, that were joined together by landfill in the mid-twentieth century. Randall's Island during the 1840s, and Wards Island from the early 1850s until 1868, collected tens of thousands of human remains from Manhattan's upturned cemeteries, the insane asylum and emigrant hospital of Wards Island and the similar institutional bedlam of Blackwell's—now Roosevelt Island—downriver. The unmarked, unmapped trenches of the Randall's and Wards Island potter's fields, discernible to the sinuses of nineteenth-century mariners passing through the East River's Hell Gate abyss, remain as such beneath the present-day homeless shelters, rehab and psychiatric centers, wastewater treatment plant, nature trails and multiple sports grounds.

In 1868, a couple of years after its brief use as a Civil War POW internment camp, the mile-long Hart Island off the northeast mainland Bronx was purchased by the city as a replacement for the Wards Island potter's field. In 2016, the *New York Times* investigated wrongdoings by court-appointed guardians and nursing homes charged with protecting ill and elderly New Yorkers, who were then lost to Hart Island's City Cemetery. Hart Island's

Hart Island circa 1890, by Jacob Riis. *Public domain.*

asylum, quarantine hospitals and boys' reformatory are now derelict ruins, whose dismantling, at the time of this writing, appears imminent. In 1985, even the dead were quarantined as seventeen new arrivals, the victims of a terrifying new disease called AIDS, were buried at the southern tip of the island, away from the graves of mixed strangers. Vast trenches, dug out by Rikers Island prisoners and overseen by New York City's Department of Correction, make up the world's largest tax-funded potter's field with over one million burials. The unlikeliest of Hart Island's residents include the novelist Dawn Powell, whose executor rejected her remains after they had undergone five years of medical study, and the Academy Award–winning Disney child star of *Peter Pan* and *Treasure Island*, Bobby Driscoll, who died in 1968 at the age of thirty-one from a drug overdose in an East Village tenement.

The Hart Island dead are buried in pine boxes, each one marked with a name or number, with the location of each burial filed on a database. Disinterment occurs when a deceased relative or friend is either found or fundraised for. The dead are delivered to the island aboard a special operations refrigerated truck that drives off the Michael Cosgrove ferry, the same ferry that on monthly visits brings the curious to an isolated gazebo area and registered mourners to the edge of a headstone-free expanse.

10

VICTORIAN INVENTIONS, TECHNIQUES AND PROCEDURES

Nineteenth-century death was well catered for and even rehearsed insofar as taking the necessary steps toward the Good Death. Literature and church instructions were readily available to teach people how to bow out gracefully and piously through prayer and preparation. At the very least, well-framed last words could secure a balcony seat in heaven. The United States penchant for refining the middle classes had strong roots in the country to which it was no longer beholden. This is evident in the American referencing of the larger part of the nineteenth century as the "Victorian era." Queen Victoria's sixty-four-year reign of the United Kingdom of Great Britain and Ireland (1837–1901) can be broadly characterized by the act of mourning. The death of her husband, Prince Albert, in 1861, prompted her to wear black for the remaining forty years of her life.

The year that Prince Albert died coincided with the beginning of a four-year onslaught of violent death that would etch itself into the framework of American life. For the soldiers lucky enough to survive the conflict of the Civil War, fatigue governed the senses, a symptom of overfamiliarity with death through witnessing it, causing it, digging shallow trenches to accommodate it and abandoning it on battlefields, scattered and putrefying. The missing, lost to muddy slaughter and confused statistics, succeeded in tarnishing the Good Death's Christian servitude. For staunch Christians, God's mysterious plan served to justify the slaughter; religion rewarded the truly committed while sacrifice safeguarded a certain paradise beyond the veil.

The Soldiers' and Sailors' Arch and the Soldiers' and Sailors' Memorial Monument in Brooklyn and Manhattan, respectively; Grand Army Plaza's gold-leafed equestrian statue of General William Tecumseh Sherman; and the zinc and bronze Union soldier statues at Green-Wood and Calvary Cemeteries go to considerable lengths in making sure that the Civil War will never be forgotten. According to *A Census-Based Count of the Civil War Dead* by Binghamton University professor J. David Hacker, published in 2011, which contests the previously accepted Union and Confederate death toll of 620,000, the number was closer to 750,000. Even the smaller estimate would put the percentage equivalent in today's U.S. population at 6.6 million. The greatest number of enlistments (approximately 460,000) and deaths (over 50,000 in the army and navy) belonged to New York State. In both the North and the South, poor sanitation, including contaminated water supplies at Union and Confederate camps, caused an untold number of civilian deaths. If fully realized, they would add a significant number to the death toll estimates. The Civil War's carnage exceeds all of the twentieth- and twenty-first-century wars combined in which the United States participated.

Civil War Monument at Calvary Cemetery in Queens.

Civil War embalming. *Public domain.*

Brooklyn-born physician Dr. Thomas Holmes observed the dilemma of death in the Civil War and filled the marketable gap with a metalloid element and a morbid handicraft that would be seized upon by entrepreneur morticians up to and beyond the present day. While pursuing the quack practice of phrenology through his study of Egyptian mummy heads, Dr. Holmes became fixated on their state of preservation. His ensuing embalming experiments led to a more sustainable death craft than the prevailing technique of zinc and poisonous mercury, which was seldom used outside of the preservation of cadavers in medical study and postmortem investigation.

Dr. Holmes developed a successful, albeit marginally less toxic method of applying arsenic to the arteries just in time for the Civil War.

Holmes's professional profile soared after his embalming of Colonel Elmer Ephraim Ellsworth, whose close friend President Lincoln described him as "the greatest little man I ever met." When the greatest little man attempted to remove a Confederate flag from the roof of an inn in Alexandria, Virginia, he was shot dead, wherefore he became the first Union officer to die in the Civil War. Holmes made the fortunes of war quite literal by upping his fee to one hundred dollars per body and showing off his adeptness by embalming random dead soldiers, plucked from the battlefield, who he then showcased at undertaker businesses in and around the nation's capital.

A vulture-like frenzy took over the Union encampments with embalmers setting up shop close by. The positioning of their trade in makeshift huts facilitated the embalming of salvageable bodies and more lucrative high-ranking military figures, many of whom were then sent by train to their families to bury as they wished. Throughout the four-year war, the embalmers' macabre trade, combined with their stalking the dead and profiting from tragedy, unnerved soldiers and civilians alike. Nonetheless, the technique picked up an elevated status with the death of Abraham Lincoln, who died from his assassination wounds just six days after Confederate general Robert E. Lee surrendered to the commanding general of the Union army and future president Ulysses S. Grant at Appomattox Courthouse (after which the war petered out in fits and spurts).

In 1862, Dr. Charles Decosta Brown, a Manhattan dentist who taught himself to be proficient in the art of embalming, was appointed to the new position of government embalmer. Three years later, Dr. Brown was given the task of embalming the president and topping up the necessary ingredients along the 1,654-mile funeral procession through 180 cities and seven states aboard the train dubbed the "Lincoln Special." Accompanying President Lincoln was his deceased son, Willie, who, having died more than three years earlier at the age of eleven from suspected typhoid fever, had been disinterred from his original burial place at Oak Hill Cemetery in Georgetown. He would be reinterred alongside his father at Springfield, Illinois, thirteen days after the Lincoln Special's departure from Washington, D.C.

A high-ranking Freemason, Dr. Brown had given the actor Edwin Booth the Third Degree—as in the ranked degree of Master Mason at the New York Lodge. Some months prior to Lincoln's assassination by Booth's younger brother and fellow actor John Wilkes Booth, Edwin had grabbed the young Robert Todd Lincoln at a train station in Jersey City and, by doing so, prevented him from slipping through the gap between the platform and a departing train. Thanks to Edwin Booth, Robert was the only one of President Lincoln's four sons to survive into adulthood.

The largest funeral procession in American history took temporary residence inside the rotunda of New York's City Hall on April 24, 1865, nine days after Lincoln's death, whereupon his remains received an unending chain of visitors who came to pay their respects. As the *New York Times* reported, "At a little after 5, Mr. Brown, the embalmer, who, skilled and competent as he is, could not be expected to form a miracle on short notice, looked at the corpse. He detected with an experienced eye the change in color and the slight falling of the lower jaw." The same article didn't hold back on identifying the frailty of Lincoln's preservation:

> *How changed in death. Those thousands who crowded zealously in the street, pushed vigorously on the stairs, strove earnestly in the corridor, glanced hastily at the face and passed hurriedly from the room, saw no Abraham Lincoln. The flurry of the crush was yet upon them when they found themselves in the presence of the dead; curiously they looked at him and instantly were gone. In this brief period phylosophical [sic] reason had no sway, the physical eye saw and reported to the mind—what? A face dark to blackness, features sharp to a miracle, an expression almost horrible in its un-nature, a stiff, starched countenance resembling none they knew of and expressive of nothing familiar. Such a sight revealed nothing of Abraham Lincoln.*

At Lincoln's funeral procession the following day, which traveled north along Broadway toward the awaiting train at Thirtieth Street, the "sixty thousand citizens in the funeral procession" and the sixteen-horse hearse passed by two small boys perched at a high window. Many years later, one of the boys would be identified in a photograph by his widow, Edith, as six-year-old future president Theodore Roosevelt, standing beside his brother, Elliott, at their grandfather Cornelius Roosevelt's Union Square mansion.

Arsenic is still present in many Civil War burial grounds. The unintentional poisoning of embalmers and the difficulty presented for postmortem investigations of intentional arsenic poisoning resulted in a ban on embalming arsenic in the early 1900s. By that time, an alternative had arrived courtesy of German chemist August Wilhelm von Hofmann, who conclusively identified formaldehyde—still the most common embalming ingredient—in the 1860s.

Lincoln funeral with six-year-old Teddy Roosevelt at the window. *Public domain.*

When Dr. Thomas Holmes died at the age of eighty-two in January 1900, his obituary in the *Brooklyn Eagle* read: "During the Civil War he embalmed 4,028 bodies. He had at his death several specimens of his embalming, of which he had made a special study for some years past. He claimed to have discovered a fluid which would destroy the germs of contagious diseases." A plaque outside of his hillside burial vault at Cypress Hills Cemetery, placed there by author and historian Andrew Carroll in 2014, pays homage to the "Father of American embalming" while informing its readers that "before Holmes was buried here in 1900, he purportedly requested that he, himself, not be embalmed." Rather than being ironic, it stands to reason that the person who knew more than anyone about the process of embalming was averse to the idea of having it applied to his own corpse. Holmes's professional rival, Professor Auguste Renouard from New Orleans, a doctor for the Confederate army, opened the Renouard Training School for Embalmers in Manhattan in 1895 and penned *The Undertaker's Manual* (1878), the first embalming textbook published in the United States.

Agencies and charitable associations, in particular the United States Christian and Sanitation Commissions, were set up to support the Union soldiers and to retrieve and log the identities of the unknown dead as best they could. On July 17, 1862, President Lincoln authorized federal spending on national cemeteries for military veterans. That same year, Cypress Hills Cemetery set aside a military section called Union Grounds. The state of New York was never a Civil War battleground, but the cemetery grew considerably to accommodate the overwhelming number of Union soldier deaths in New York hospitals.

Fort Schuyler in the Bronx; Governors, Bedloe's, Hart, Wards, Rikers and Davids Islands; and even the Tombs—Manhattan's notorious city jail—became POW internment camps for the Confederates. Due to prison conditions, the death toll mounted. The majority of those who were buried on the POW islands were eventually reinterred at Cypress Hills, even though Confederate soldiers were not included in the United States National Cemetery System. In 1906, an act was passed that authorized grave markers for the Confederate dead. Though similar, the top of the Union grave marker is rounded and the Confederate grave pointed, and the Union shield is, of course, absent from the Confederate marker. The Civil War dead of Cypress Hills are rare in that the Union soldier majority of over three thousand are mixed together with almost five hundred Confederate prisoners.

Cypress Hills National Cemetery is the only one of its kind in New York City. Its white domino headstone rows are divided into three sections. In addition to the Union Grounds in Cypress Hills Cemetery, in 1941, New York State donated the Mount of Victory plot to the National Cemetery. The oldest person buried there is Hiram Cronk, who joined the War of 1812 as a drummer boy. No stranger to malt whiskey and tobacco, Cronk made himself comfortable for the entire stretch of the nineteenth century. His death at the age of 105 in 1905 made him the last surviving veteran of the War of 1812. For his longevity and service, he was honored with a state funeral. As his coffin journeyed from Grand Central Station to City Hall to lie in state, the *Sun* observed, "From remarks made along the route of the funeral procession there seemed to be an impressive amount of ignorance among the populace as to whose funeral it was."

The geographically separate Cypress Hills National Cemetery—the third section—was constructed in the mid-1880s less than a mile away from the original Cypress Hills Cemetery. The combined twenty-one thousand veterans, civilians and Medal of Honor recipients of the three cemetery sections fought in just about every major war that America has been involved with up until the mid-twentieth century. Revolutionary War veterans reinterred from older defunct graveyards are the oldest of the cemetery's residents. Even though the National Cemetery reached capacity in 1954, the burial of family members in existing plots occurs from time to time.

In 1926, Cypress Hills National Cemetery received around one thousand reinterments from Brooklyn Naval Hospital Cemetery at Wallabout Bay. The hospital site, currently occupied by the film and TV soundstages of Steiner Studios, is listed on the National Register of Historic Places. Its cemetery, now the Brooklyn Waterfront Greenway's 1.7-acre Naval Cemetery Landscape, still retains somewhere up to one thousand unmarked graves.

Edward Perry Vollum, promoted to surgeon, lieutenant colonel and medical inspector in the second year of the Civil War, was not only overly

Cypress Hills National Cemetery in Brooklyn. *Author's photo with permission of the National Cemetery Association.*

familiar with death but also wary of its diagnosis. Presumed dead from drowning in a childhood accident, Vollum escaped burial after regaining consciousness in the nick of time. Taphophobia, the fear of being buried alive, is reported to be among the most common phobias, and it is not without merit. A lack of understanding regarding how a corpse can swell and contort and change position is likely to have warped any available data, but paralysis, comas, quack doctors and shocking errors aroused a persistent fear of premature burial throughout the nineteenth century.

English reformers William Tebb and Walter Hadwen, active campaigners for the prevention of animal cruelty, slavery, alcohol consumption and vaccines, were also, not unreasonably, anti–premature burial. In 1896, Tebb and Hadwen went about forming the London Association for the Prevention of Premature Burial, which promoted safety coffins and a thorough medical checkup in the event of assumed death. That same year, perhaps as a companion piece, Tebb, Hadwen and their associate Vollum put together an anecdotal manual of sorts called *Premature Burial and How It May Be Prevented.* The book describes several unpleasant New York–based episodes, including one that takes place in Brooklyn around the year of 1851. When a girl named Virginia Macdonald, who lived with her father, fell sick and then died, her mother, unconvinced of Virginia's death, had her exhumed from her grave at Green-Wood Cemetery. Virginia was discovered lying on her side with severely bitten hands, apparent evidence of having died *after* her burial.

On December 5, 1882, J.G. Krichbaum from Ohio received a patent for his "Device For Life In Buried Persons." Aside from providing oxygen, Krichbaum's design consisted of a movable periscope-type pipe that could indicate, if pushed or rotated by the person inside, that all was not well, or rather that the person inside was well enough, and not dead. Krichbaum's patent pitch—that his invention is "that class of devices for indicating life in buried persons"—suggests that inventions of this kind were not so rare. On July 3, 1900, in Buffalo, New York, in a reverse type of invention to fellow Buffalo resident Alfred P. Southwick's electric chair, Walter J. McKnight patented an "Electric Device for Indicating the Awakening of Persons Buried Alive." The device included a breathing pipe that was to be inserted into the casket, a "house or box-like structure" above the grave and an electric signal for the "supposed corpse" to sound the alarm to the land of the living. Safety coffins were devised to prevent premature burial, although there is no evidence that any have ever been successful.

In the presence of trained twenty-first-century professionals equipped with rigorous life-detecting medical tools, one would think that premature burial is a thing of the past. Unfortunately, this isn't so. In 2014, in Thessaloniki, Greece, a woman who had just been buried was heard screaming by children playing close by. She died of asphyxia before the authorities were able to dig her out of her premature grave. In August 2020, a Michigan woman, declared dead by paramedics, was discovered very much alive by funeral home staff who were just about to embalm her. In January 2021, in the city of Resistencia, Argentina, an eighty-nine-year-old woman was saved in the nick of time when her daughter detected vital signs just seconds before she was about to be cremated.

An unsavory episode such as Virginia Macdonald's alleged premature burial wasn't going to hinder the success of Green-Wood Cemetery, which was—according to Selden C. Judson's 1881 guide *The Cemeteries of New York, and How to Reach Them*—"the first Cemetery of the United States." For nineteenth-century New Yorkers, Green-Wood Cemetery represented a range of possibilities and self-expression that freed them up from the constraints of the pew

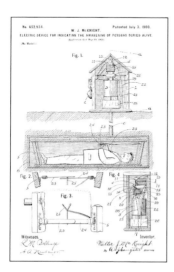

W.J. McKnight's safety coffin patent. *Public domain.*

Van Ness Parsons mausoleum at the Green-Wood Cemetery in Brooklyn. *Author's photo with permission of the Green-Wood Cemetery.*

and of dull, uniform convention. By the mid-nineteenth century, Green-Wood, a tangle of passages built around the natural ascent of Battle Hill, the highest point of Brooklyn and a strategic point in the 1776 Battle of Brooklyn, was one of the most visited tourist attractions in America.

Incorporated in 1838, Green-Wood Cemetery transpired as a result of the vision and clout of Henry Evelyn Pierrepont, a real estate businessman, city planner and social organizer, and the joint effort of two cities, New York and Brooklyn. Today, Green-Wood Cemetery has the second highest number of interments (over half a million) and the largest number of cemetery acres (478) in New York City. The wealthy merchant Schermerhorn family sold their grazing land to Green-Wood as additional cemetery space, which the family then used to build their magnificent mausoleums. Peter Schermerhorn's Egyptian Revival tomb is large enough to house the deceased in their dozens.

Many of the designers responsible for Green-Wood's beauty, such as John LaFarge and Louis Comfort Tiffany, are buried there also, as are an improbable mix of exceptional and singular people: hot dog inventor Charles Feltman; the Soda Fountain King John Matthews; Morse code man Samuel Morse and his family of Oliver Cromwell's descendants; Laura Keene, the lead actress in *Our American Cousin*, watched by President Lincoln on the

Inside the Thomas Durant mausoleum at the Green-Wood Cemetery in Brooklyn. *Author's photo with permission of the Green-Wood Cemetery.*

night of his assassination; Do-Hum-Me, the eighteen-year-old daughter of a Sauk chief and a P.T. Barnum American Museum performer; and New York Nativist and gangster William Poole, better known as Bill the Butcher.

The New Burying Ground in New Haven, Connecticut (later called Grove Street Cemetery), incorporated in 1797, was private, nonsectarian and the first chartered cemetery in the United States. Mount Auburn Cemetery in Cambridge, Massachusetts, dedicated in 1831, was the first rural cemetery in the United States and greatly inspired the rest of the country to follow suit. Gothic, Greek and Egyptian Revival design and the landscape composition of rolling hills and lakes influenced by the vast country estates of England came to represent social status as well as a place to breathe fresh air outside of noxious city life. Trolleys, horses and buggies lent themselves to the act of sightseeing, while new extended train travel and ferry services brought visitors from long distances and across rivers.

Frederick Law Olmsted and Calvert Vaux would alleviate the numbers who had come to rely on rural cemeteries for leisure with their creation of Central and Prospect Parks in the 1850–60s. Among those who inspired them was the romantic figure of Andrew Jackson Downing, a pioneer of landscape design who fashioned the Evergreens Cemetery in Brooklyn in the late-1840s and whose life was cut short at the age of thirty-six by the sinking of the *Henry Clay* steamboat that caught fire on the Hudson in 1852. There is a decadent rakishness to Downing's Evergreens, not as shiny as its past, beauty without polish, a mixture of class and corrosion. As a tribute to him, Olmsted and Vaux named a park after him in Newburgh, New York, and Vaux named his son Downing. Tragedy continued, however, with the drowning of Calvert Vaux at Brooklyn's Gravesend Bay, and later, his son Downing's suicide from jumping off a YMCA roof in Kingston.

In 1835, a Greek Revival house on Manhattan's East Fourth Street was purchased by Seabury Tredwell of the successful hardware company Tredwell, Kissam, & Co. After moving in with his wife and seven children, his eighth and final child, Gertrude, was born in the house in 1840. When Seabury died in an upstairs bedroom in 1865, his funeral was held in the parlor—derived from the French verb *parler*, meaning "to speak." The function of the parlor was social, including when a member of the household died, and people would come and pay their respects. For this reason, the parlor was also called the death room. When death became less frequent and the blossoming death-care industry began to swiftly shift the body from the home to the funeral parlor, the original parlor, the death room, became the living room.

Seabury Tredwell's remaining family members lived at home into old age. Gertrude, the last to die, having never married since her father had disapproved of her one and only suitor, lived alone for the last twenty-four years of her life and kept the house exactly as it had been during the nineteenth century. After Gertrude's death at the age of ninety-three in 1933, a cousin saved the house from demolition. In 1936, the only known Victorian house in New York City to have all of its original family possessions opened up as the Merchant's House Museum. Gertrude's solitary old-fashioned presence in the community was distinct enough to linger long after her death in the stories that continue to sustain Greenwich Village ghost tourism.

Superstition was a ubiquitous distraction in the Victorian era. Efforts to communicate with the dead were well-practiced before and after the Civil War, but esoteric pastimes, in a departure from old-fashioned magical beliefs, became elevated by pseudoscientific experimentation. The new wandering herds that got off at the various stops of the Erie Canal were looking to craft their own folklores. The Burned-over District of western New York isolated its Second Awakening visions and ideas before sending them out like freight, back along the Erie Canal to New York City and beyond: Mormonism, Millerism (which culminated in a momentous nonevent called the Great Disappointment, called so because William Miller's prediction that the Second Coming would appear on October 22, 1844, was incorrect) and the rapping medium Fox Sisters (the shared headstone of Margaretta and Catherine Fox at Cypress Hills Cemetery labels their respective death dates as a "transition"). Transcendentalism and mesmerism from New England and Europe blended with the magic lantern mysteries of daguerreotype photographs and electrical telegraphy. Shifts in social class empowered women to immerse themselves in spiritualism. A more inquisitive, personal relationship with religion emerged from the middle and upper classes, who found comfort and excitement in clairvoyance and met in private homes for séances and at venues and summer camps for spiritualist lectures and demonstrations.

One of the most significant of the camp meeting locations was Lily Dale, a tiny hamlet in western New York founded in 1879 by members of the spiritualist movement. Lily Dale spiritualism, as exemplified by wellness industry endorsements and an HBO documentary, has become big business. Similarly, in New York City, psychics have woven themselves into the five boroughs with the brashness of twenty-four-hour pharmacies. Since 1967, the act of fortune-telling has been effectively banned. New York State's penal law definition of fortune-telling is a "class B misdemeanor" that pertains to

> *claimed or pretended use of occult powers, to answer questions or give advice on personal matters or to exorcise, influence or affect evil spirits or curses; except that this section does not apply to a person who engages in the aforedescribed conduct as part of a show or exhibition solely for the purpose of entertainment or amusement.*

Michael Wilson of the *New York Times* addressed this conundrum in 2011: "A law that protects evil spirits: only in New York." In the legal framework of the state, New York psychics must present themselves as entertainers with a disclaimer that clarifies that the readings shouldn't be taken too seriously. The convenient confidentiality of fortune-telling can easily evade this, and customers may therefore be vulnerable to a mysterious domain in which fun and fraud are playful bedfellows. According to a query put forth by *Vice* magazine to the State Department of Labor and in keeping with the enigmatic nature of the fortune-telling trade, within the "Entertainers and Performers" tax category, psychics are listed as "other."

Henry Steel Olcott, the densely bearded special commissioner and colonel to the War and Navy Departments during the Civil War, was also a lawyer, journalist, Buddhist convert and leader—along with Russian mystic and philosopher Madame (Helena) Blavatsky—of the Theosophical Society, which materialized in a Manhattan apartment in 1875. The society molded together Hellenistic philosophy, Eastern religions and occultism with "elementary spirits." This ideological group hug may have kickstarted all things New Age, but one of its first noteworthy happenings was the incineration of an early Theosophical Society member, Joseph Henry Louis Charles de Palm, whose Bavarian baronial heritage afforded him the title Baron de Palm.

Olcott, the executor of de Palm's will and the recipient of much of his estate (which turned out to be meager), had suggested cremation when the dying de Palm asked Olcott for advice on how best to dispose of his body. Following de Palm's death in May 1876, his embalmed body was stored in the receiving tomb of the Lutheran (now All Faiths) Cemetery. Ahead of the cremation, an act that was abhorrent to most God-fearing Americans, de Palm's funeral ceremony at New York's Masonic Temple added fuel to the fire due to the negative press coverage. By this time, the budding New York Cremation Society had turned its back on the intended proceedings. The Theosophical Society's spiritual and meditative practices must have come in handy for the six months that Olcott was encumbered with Baron de Palm's corpse, which, throughout its waiting game on ice, had endured a couple of embalming missteps that including being stuffed with potter's clay.

At last, it came to be known that a doctor named Francis Julius LeMoyne, located near Washington, Pennsylvania, had constructed a crematory in response to what he believed was a poisoned water supply caused by decomposing human remains in the local cemeteries. The fact that LeMoyne had tested his furnace only on sheep was good enough for Alcott, who traveled west and summoned the press to what would be a historic event, one where he could finally rid himself of his rotting clay-filled plus-one appendage. On December 6, 1876, at the LeMoyne Crematory on Gallows Hill, in the company of reporters, health board representatives and curious and bawdy locals, Baron de Palm became the first person to receive a modern cremation in the United States. Making reference to the rowdy onlookers, the *New York Times* remarked, "They would have behaved similarly if the occasion had been the hanging of a murderer, instead of the burning of a theosophist of a high degree."

An ancient practice and a common ritual of the selected faiths of Asia, cremation was nonetheless viewed as radical and even barbaric in Baron de Palm's time and region, but gradually, the United States became accustomed to cremation's sanitary briskness and economic restraint.

There are four crematoriums in New York City: at Woodlawn Cemetery in the Bronx; Green-Wood Cemetery in Brooklyn; St. Michael's Cemetery in

Fresh Pond Crematory, 1924.
Queens Public Library.

Elmhurst, Queens; and one of the oldest in the United States—Fresh Pond Crematory in Middle Village—also in Queens. (There was once a crematorium in Manhattan in the basement of the castle-like New York Cancer Hospital, which opened in 1887 on Central Park West. It was the first cancer hospital in the United States and is now a luxury apartment building.) On December 4, 1885, Eugene Lievre, an Austrian hotelier from Hoboken, became Fresh Pond's first human cremation (like LeMoyne Crematory, it had tested the mechanism with sheep). A blunder occurred when the undertaker's assistant struggled with the hook of the door to the retort. Before it was successfully shut, the family of the deceased and the crowd of spectators witnessed the cloth covering the body burst into flames.

When Wagnerian conductor Anton Seidl died of food poisoning, aged forty-seven, in 1898, his well-attended public memorial service at the Metropolitan Opera House was dutifully followed by his cremation at Fresh Pond Crematory. Once his body had entered the retort, female fans swarmed his casket to grab at "souvenir" flowers. Today, Seidl's ashes occupy a heavyweight position at the columbarium, inside an urn that doubles as a museum piece. Made of white marble and depicting allegorical scenes of life, death and music, it was designed by renowned sculptor George Grey Barnard, whose earlier three-foot-tall version, deemed too large by Seidl's widow, is on display at the Carnegie Museum of Art in Pittsburgh, Pennsylvania, and titled *Urn of Life*.

II

DEATH GRIP

Allen Durfee, born in Palmyra, Wayne County, in western New York in 1829, the same place that produced Joseph Smith's Latter-day Saint movement and *The Book of Mormon*, relocated as an adult to Grand Rapids, Michigan, where he began his career as an undertaker. He then organized a state convention of the Funeral Directors of Michigan and was elected as its president. The state group soon gave rise to the very first National Funeral Directors Association (NFDA) convention in Rochester, New York in 1882. Now the world's largest network of funeral industry professionals, the NFDA has its very own podcast, *A Brush with Death*, and an online store where members can purchase book titles such as *Why Facebook Works for Funeral Homes: And Everything Else Doesn't!* After the formation of the NFDA, Durfee went about selling his very own Durfee Embalming Fluid via traveling salesmen and casket companies all over America.

Today, a casket outsourced beyond the funeral home variety, from, for instance, the Batesville Casket Company—a subsidiary of plastic industry behemoths Hillenbrand Inc.—or Walmart's Overnight Caskets (presumably a reference to delivery time rather than the shortchanging of eternal rest) can be just as expensive.

Adding to the list of unnecessary costs, embalming is sometimes applied even when there isn't an open casket funeral, at a time when grieving families are paying less attention to the billing of services than they normally would. Most funeral homes have sufficient refrigeration for an alternative preservation method. As for concerns about sanitation, the average dead body is not contagious. Outside of North America, embalming with formaldehyde didn't used to be commonplace, but in the countries where the American death-care industry has heavily invested, its usage has shown a marked increase in recent years.

The purpose of embalming is to make the deceased look as close to their living self as possible for the duration of the funeral. After the blood and remaining bodily fluids are drained from the deceased via their arteries and abdominal cavity, they are replaced with formalin, a formaldehyde solution mixed with water and methanol. Meanwhile, the eyelids and mouth are sealed shut with the aid of sewing, gluing and/or wiring. Although the process is effective in delaying the process of decomposition, when the inevitable occurs, the embalming chemicals will leak into the earth and any nearby channels of water. Like arsenic, formaldehyde is also a carcinogen. The Occupational Safety and Health Administration, an agency of the United States Department of Labor, instituted restrictions on the use of formaldehyde in the workplace in the 1980s. In December 2019, the Environmental Protection Agency designated formaldehyde as a "High Priority Substance" under the Toxic Substances Control Act. At the time of writing, the chemical is undergoing risk evaluation.

If an award existed for the most opaque business title, then Service Corporation International, the leading U.S. provider of funeral, cemetery and cremation goods and services, would be a deserving winner. Founded by Robert L. Waltrip in 1962 and headquartered in Houston, Texas, SCI has consumed the death-care industry by quietly purchasing existing funeral homes and cemeteries all over North America. Its brand titles include Dignity Memorial, Dignity Planning, Funeraria del Angel, Memorial Plan, the National Cremation Society and the Neptune Society. For decades, SCI competed with two other death-care industry giants, Stewart Enterprises and the Loewen Group (which became the Alderwoods Group after bankruptcy). Today, SCI owns both of them.

Jessica Mitford, distinguishable among the famous English Mitford sisters for belonging to the nonfascist camp, wrote a witty and thorough critique of the American death-care industry in her 1963 bestselling book, *The American Way of Death*. Mitford completed an updated version of the book called *The American Way of Death Revisited* just before her own death in 1996. In both versions, she discusses the monopolization of the American funeral industry by SCI and the financial pitfalls encountered by the average customer. The huge reaction to Mitford's 1963 book from fervid letter writers who had unwittingly found themselves backed into a funeral corner with an extortionate price tag made her a popular dartboard bull's-eye figure for the National Funeral Directors Association.

Aside from being a significant irritation to the funeral industry, Mitford's book was also a rallying cry for the investigation that was to be carried out by the Federal Trade Commission's Bureau of Consumer Protection. On April 30, 1984, after many years of toing and froing with Congress and a long battle with the funeral industry, the FTC was able to enact the Funeral Rule, which stipulates that funeral businesses must provide clear information and an itemized list of services to consumers and that a customer has the right to choose only the goods and services that they want or need.

As a National Public Radio investigation found in February 2017, funeral home service prices can differ by thousands of dollars depending on which one a person happens to walk into, even when the majority of them offer the exact same services, operate in the same geographical area or, in the case of cremation, use the same crematorium. In March 2017, a press release from the Consumer Federation of America and the Funeral Consumer Alliance reported that as well as refusing to disclose their prices, SCI operations' median prices were up to 72 percent higher than other funeral homes. SCI favors package deals with all the trimmings and trappings that a customer really should not have to expect for such an occasion.

The Funeral Rule, enacted in the pre-internet era, specified the right to receive price information on the telephone and a written itemized price list in person. Since 1984, most funeral services are still outrageously expensive and nonessential add-ons have become the norm. In the NPR investigative piece, a legal representative for the NFDA justified the variety of funeral costs by making a comparison with the purchase of burgers or weddings, selected according to the quality of service provided. Unlike the pursuit of calories or nuptials, the average grieving funeral customer does not have the time or the inclination to shop around, change their mind or cancel.

In June 2020, in response to the FTC's request for comments, the Funeral Consumers Alliance reported the following:

> *Funeral homes routinely refused to disclose their prices, or to offer consistent prices in writing to grieving families.*
>
> *Funeral homes compelled families to buy all-inclusive packages, what the industry refers to as a "traditional" funeral.*
>
> *Consumers were not permitted to buy services such as embalming, calling hours, a graveside service, and others item by item. The cost of the casket often included "all our customary services."*

Funeral home staff frequently misled consumers by falsely claiming, for example, that embalming was a legally required purchase when that was not the case.

The same report revealed that "in years of research on funeral home prices, we have yet to find one SCI funeral home that discloses its prices on its website."

At the turn of the twenty-first century, an antitrust action led by the attorney general of New York, Eliot Spitzer, resulted in SCI selling a number of funeral homes at the behest of concerned Jewish communities. One of the funeral homes, the Plaza Memorial Chapel (now the Plaza Jewish Community Chapel) on the Upper West Side, was sold under pressure to a group of Jewish philanthropic organizations. As the chapel's present-day website reports, it is "owned and operated by the Jewish Community as a service rather than a business."

Many high-profile Washington, D.C. funerals including those of Senator John McCain and Presidents Gerald Ford, Ronald Regan and George H.W. Bush, have been presided over by Robert M. Boetticher Sr., who is currently the assistant vice president to the founder and chairman emeritus of SCI and president and CEO of LHT (Legacy Honor Trust) Consulting Group, which is a subsidiary of SCI. *Presidential Funerals* and *George H.W. Bush Memorial Exhibit* are on permanent exhibition at the National Museum of Funeral History in Houston, Texas. Founded in 1992 by SCI founder and longtime CEO (until 2015) Robert Waltrip, the museum shares a campus with Waltrip's Commonwealth Institute of Funeral Service, a death-care industry training school that prepares its students for careers within SCI.

Multiple lawsuits and even one managerial-level suicide have nipped at SCI's heels over the years, but thus far, SCI has successfully managed to stamp out scandal with multimillion-dollar out-of-court settlements. The various filed suits pertain to SCI funeral homes and cemeteries dumping the deceased in the woods; destroying vaults; mixing body parts to make room for other bodies; burying a stillborn in an eight-inch shallow grave; leaving two hundred bodies "on makeshift gurneys in the garage, in hallways and in a back room, unrefrigerated and leaking fluids onto the floor" per the *Washington Post*; and "Funeralgate," called so because of the sudden firing of the Texas Funeral Service Commission executive director Eliza May during her investigation into unlicensed embalmers. In 1999, May hit back by filing a whistleblower lawsuit against the State of Texas, SCI and Robert Waltrip, alleging that all of the above together with Texas governor George W. Bush,

Rudolph Valentino's funeral in Manhattan. *Public domain.*

who by then had joined the presidential race, had deliberately thwarted her investigation because of Republican donor Waltrip's friendship with Bush's father, former president George H.W. Bush. The lawsuit ended in an out-of-court settlement in 2001. In December 2019, California attorney general Xavier Becerra sued the Neptune Society, a national provider of cremation services and a subsidiary of SCI, for allegedly pocketing $100 million from prepaid cremation customers. SCI has traded on the New York Stock Exchange since 1974, and like all good dastardly corporations, its modus operandi can be traced all the way to the top.

Frank Campbell, born on the Fourth of July 1872, introduced the first funeral parlor chapel, the Frank E. Campbell Burial and Cremation Company, to New York in 1898. Campbell was also the first to put the funeral procession on motorized wheels. When Italian matinée idol Rudolph Valentino died of a perforated ulcer at age thirty-one in 1926, Campbell took full advantage. His hiring of actors to play security in the guise of Benito Mussolini's Blackshirts and the staging of hysterical grieving stoked the mass hysteria already present as thousands of fans gathered outside the Saint Malachy Catholic Church on West Forty-Ninth Street for Valentino's funeral. The reported frenzy, injuries and grief-stricken suicides provided Campbell with business-boosting headlines. The present-day Frank E. Campbell Funeral Chapel is still the most sought-after and expensive funeral organizer in the city. Its star-studded funerals have included those of James Cagney, Joan Crawford, Judy Garland, George Gershwin, Rita Hayworth,

Frank E. Campbell Funeral Chapel in Manhattan.

Robert F. Kennedy, John Lennon, Mae West, Heath Ledger, Jackie Onassis, Philip Seymour Hoffman, Tennessee Williams, Nikola Tesla, Greta Garbo and Joan Rivers.

At the Cemetery Belt's Beth Olam Cemetery, on a white marble plaque nailed to the gatepost, is an antiquated advertisement for the services of Charles Rosenthal, who was once the sexton for Shaaray Tefila's West End synagogue and funeral director for the Riverside Memorial Chapel on the Upper West Side. Rosenthal entered the funeral business in 1897 and was instrumental in developing the modern funeral home model. His grandson Edward Rosenthal, who took over the business and acquired multiple funeral homes, including New York showbusiness favorite the Frank E. Campbell Funeral Chapel, formed a car rental business with his son-in-law Steve Ross that made extracurricular use of their funeral vehicles. They then merged the funeral company with the New Jersey mobster-owned Kinney Parking Company, which then became the multitask Kinney Service. Having undergone many guises and acquisitions, in 1969 they purchased the entertainment company Warner Bros.–Seven Arts Def Inc., which morphed into Warner Communications. The resulting merger in 1990 was Time Warner (today's multinational mass-media corporation WarnerMedia), of which Steve Ross became CEO. In 1971, one year before Edward Rosenthal commenced his position as vice chairman of Warner Communications, he sold his funeral business to death-care industry overlords Service Corporation

International, which now owns Riverside Memorial Chapel and the Frank E. Campbell Funeral Chapel.

All in all, the average funeral and burial cost with all the trimmings in New York City is in excess of $8,000. Like airlines and cinemas, cemeteries make money from add-ons. The type of casket, embalming, hearse, transportation fee, grave liner, grave marker and memorial and graveside services are the funeral equivalent of popcorn and a reclining chair. No law requires a casket for burial or cremation, but individual cemeteries have their own rules. A burial vault or grave liner is an outer shell for the casket, which according to most sales pitches will provide extra security for your loved one. Commonly made from concrete, the grave liner's authentic purpose is to aid the smooth ride of a lawnmower by preventing the ground from sinking into the disintegration of the deceased and their casket.

"Endowed Care" stickers on graves are a common cemetery feature. They signify perpetual care for the upkeep of individual plots or columbarium niches. Perpetual care is distinct from permanent care. According to the New York State Association of Cemeteries:

> *The laws of New York require all regulated cemeteries to take 10% of every sale and $35 from each burial and place it in a managed Permanent Maintenance Fund. As a cemetery continues to sell property, this fund grows considerably. Once there is no more property to sell, the income from the Permanent Maintenance Fund is used to maintain the cemetery in perpetuity.*

In 2007, when the current archbishop of New York, Timothy Dolan, was the archbishop of Milwaukee, he wrote a letter to the Vatican, requesting that approximately $55 million in funds be shifted into an archdiocese perpetual care cemetery trust fund. After several years of listening to victims during the Catholic Church sexual abuse investigations, and a few weeks ahead of the Wisconsin Supreme Court's ruling that would allow sexual abuse victims to make a claim against the archdiocese, Dolan penned the letter that included the following sentence: "By transferring these assets to the trust, I foresee an improved protection of these funds from any legal claim and liability." The Vatican responded to the letter by approving the transfer. In March 2015, a federal appeals court reinstated a lawsuit that could pursue those cemetery funds on behalf of the victims, which had previously been prohibited as a result of the Archdiocese of Milwaukee's bankruptcy case.

Mitford's two books make mention of religious resistance to death-care industry exploitation with instances of the clergy accompanying the bereaved to the funeral home to safeguard their purchase of a reasonably priced casket. But contrary to their previous stance that stood at loggerheads with mainstream death-care industry costs, religion-affiliated interment prices are no longer so cost-effective. The Catholic Cemeteries of the Roman Catholic Diocese of Brooklyn price list is only attainable after making an appointment with a family services counselor. The Archdiocese of New York has an online price list for the minutiae that exists outside of a memorial service and body disposal options. Their average cost for Calvary Cemetery, including foundation and monument permit fees, perpetual and annual care fees, grave and crypt opening fees (for adding a family member) and "other" service fees is around $8,000. Meanwhile, Saint Raymond's grave sites in the Bronx sell at around $5,500–$6,000. Grave opening fees cost almost $3,000, while a onetime payment of $980 for the perpetual care program will ensure trimmed grass. The Saint Raymond's website, where the price list is available, is run by eCatholic, the largest provider of Catholic websites in the United States. Its founder and CEO, Josh Simmons, refers to his transition from a Catholic youth minister to a web design entrepreneur as his "Peter moment." Like Saint Peter, who walked on water after hearing Jesus say: "Take courage, it is I; do not be afraid," Simmons acted on an echo of this sound advice and promptly left the church ministry for a career in church-affiliated tech.

The premium cost of moving with the times is inescapable and applies to the nondenominational-turned-nonsectarian cemeteries of New York City. To be interred at the prestigious Green-Wood Cemetery can cost the same as a down payment on real estate. Green Wood's cremation costs, however, are surprisingly reasonable.

Some New York synagogues offer burial plots as a right of membership, but Jewish New York City cemetery interment, maintenance and grave opening fees can ascend quickly into the thousands.

More than 4,000 cemeteries in New York State are religious, municipal, familial or private. The other 1,900-plus cemeteries are not-for-profit organizations that are regulated by the New York State Division of Cemeteries, which oversees their establishment, maintenance and burial ground preservation. Not-for-profit cemeteries can charge different amounts for their individual services, but any change in fees must be requested from and then permitted by the Cemetery Board. Composed of the secretary of state, the Department of Law and the Department of Health or their designees, the Cemetery Board supervises the Division of Cemeteries.

Crematory in use. *Wikimedia Commons.*

According to the market and consumer data company Statista, the cremation rate in the United States reached 54.6 percent in 2019 and is projected to grow to 79.1 by 2035. In some American crematories, the room containing the ovens adjoins the chapel where funeral services take place. The assembled mourners can then view the passage of the coffin into the retort through a glass partition, after which the retort door is shut. When the incineration is over, the reduced bones and elemental fragments are then pulverized by a grinding machine called a cremulator into ashes, or cremains.

For those who have money to burn, alternative, symbolic or mind-boggling tributes are on the rise and can be catered for in selected areas of the United States. Cremation ashes can lend themselves to tattoos, jewelry, paintings, fireworks, reef balls, Earth-orbiting rockets and even ammunition designed specifically to shoot wild turkeys.

In New York City, the cost of direct cremation lingers in the hundreds, with variables that depend on attendance and location. The death-care industry has a tendency to draw customers toward a range of combustible caskets, urns and columbarium niches. An individual niche, including its design, font, the type of urn that sits inside of it and its whereabouts within a columbarium can run up the price ladder into multiple thousands. The thrifty option, of course, is to take the ashes home or scatter them. The quandary the columbarium business will more often than not put forth in defense of the niche is that when the cycle of life ends for the generational caretakers of the homespun urn full of ashes, then what will become of the urn? The truth is that in such a scenario, the fate of an urn with no takers hardly matters.

According to the Environmental Protection Agency, cremations were responsible for 5.5 percent of the nation's mercury emissions in 2017 due to the burning of dental fillings. The propensity to scatter ashes on fertile land in order to maintain the continuity of a person's life can be misguided. Unlike buried bodies, ashes don't decompose and the sodium content can be harmful to plant life unless the ashes are distributed in small amounts. State, city and park guidelines apply for scattering ashes on land that isn't privately owned, or sea, where ashes should be scattered at least three nautical miles from shore. The large number of deaths from COVID-19 in the spring of 2020 and the ensuing high number of cremations were a concern to the environmental monitors of New York City. As a consequence of the pandemic, the need for swift disposal has endured. For all its environmental liabilities and its price-jacking by the death-care industry, cremation continues to satisfy the dueling demands of space and cost, two restless issues on the minds of most New York City residents.

EPILOGUE

Apart from the distinguished or notorious few, the rest of us are likely to be forgotten within three, maybe four generations if we're lucky. Life moves on. The most populous city in the United States, New York City is home to more than 8.4 million people and over 40 percent of New York State's population (19.4 million). There are nearly 400,000 more women than men in New York City, with a gender ratio of 91.2 men to 100 women. 14.5 percent of New Yorkers are over the age of 65, with an average life expectancy of 81.2 years, faring better than the 78.6 years national average. Due to New York's aging population, within the next decade, the number of deaths is expected to rise significantly. On average, there is a New York birth every 4.4 minutes and a death every 9.1 minutes.

During the first New York coronavirus spike in March/April 2020, the sight of refrigerated death trucks became commonplace in many neighborhoods as morgues and funeral homes reached maximum capacity. Some overwhelmed funeral homes were helped by Hands with a Heart, led by Professor David Penepent from the Funeral Services Administration Department at the State University of New York in Canton, a 350-plus-mile drive from the city. Penepent and his students organized the transportation of bodies to crematories beyond the city and to other states. An additional hardship was the mandated reduction of gatherings at funerals so as to comply with social distancing rules. As of 2021, FEMA (Federal Emergency Management Agency) has provided financial assistance for COVID-19-related funeral expenses backdated to the beginning of the

Refrigerated COVID-19 truck on Randall's Island.

pandemic. While epidemics and pandemics are dependable agents for accelerating science and sanitation, the coronavirus media coverage in New York City regularly covered the same issue: a lack of space.

DeathLAB, a team of Columbia University professors and researchers, philosophers, scholars, architects and designers, has been working on strategies to ease the problem of space and environmental damage caused by common burials and cremation. One of the proposed solutions is a short-term energy-converting network of shrines called Constellation Park that would transform individual biomass from the deceased into 'mourning lights" under the Manhattan Bridge. Platforms and walkways beneath the bridge would allow people to visit the vessels. When the bodies in each vessel have fully decomposed after about a year, the individual lights would extinguish, and each vessel would become available again.

There is a growing market for more ecofriendly biocremations. Alkaline hydrolysis (originally patented in 1888 for "the treatment of bones and animal waste"), which is legal—though not necessarily practiced—in approximately two-fifths of the United States, is a process by which the human body is dissolved in heated water and lye. At the end of the process, separate from the bones that are turned into ash, the sterile liquid is either flushed down the drain or used for other purposes (such as watering the lawn), depending on state laws. For those who are averse to the down-the-drain method, it should be noted that the fluids drained from the body during the embalming process are often disposed of in the same way. In 2012, a New York Assembly bill titled "Authorizes the use of alkaline hydrolysis tissue digestion process for the disposal of cadavers and human tissue used for medical education," somewhat fittingly—with regards to the legal jargon—died in committee.

Green burials, where the unembalmed body is buried in a biodegradable casket or just a shroud (basically the same as the Muslim way of death), are becoming increasingly popular. A growing number of cemeteries in New York State, including Green-Wood Cemetery in the city, can accommodate green burials.

Constellation Park, view from riverbank, designed by Columbia GSAPP DeathLAB and LATENT Productions. *Permission granted by DeathLAB.*

Recompose, a public benefit corporation death-care service based in Washington State and founded by designer and entrepreneur Katrina Spade, is providing a practical solution to shrinking burial space and cemetery and cremation pollution. The Recompose method is as thus: after the body is placed inside a vessel, an oxygenated recipe of woodchips and alfalfa turn the body into a "nutrient-dense soil" in thirty days. The result, no longer the residue of human DNA, is one cubic yard of soil amendment. The family and friends of the deceased can then collect the compost and do with it as they wish—divide it, store it, donate it and/or put it to use in the garden. For those who aren't completely sold on the idea, they can at least yield to the ecofriendly consequences: no space invading, no carcinogens, no carbon emissions, no casket or coffin. As with a number of progressive life and death issues such as assisted suicide, the Pacific Northwest leads again. Recompose got the green light in 2020 when Washington became the first state to legalize natural organic reduction with a bill that passed with bipartisan majority in the House and the Senate.

The quality of life for the dying has improved also. Part of the impetus for British nurse Dame Cicely Saunders's devising of the modern hospice system in London came from falling in love with two dying patients, although not at the same time. The combination of her lectures on palliative care in 1960s America and the work of Swiss American writer and psychiatrist Elisabeth Kübler-Ross, in particular her 1969 bestseller *On Death and Dying*, paved the way for the Medicare Hospice Benefit that was passed by Congress in 1982.

The Death Positive movement, whose aim is to demystify death, is promoted and supported by a number of groups and organizations, including the Order of the Good Death, founded in 2011 by mortician and author Caitlin Doughty, and Morbid Anatomy, an online forum of historical and scientific talks, workshops and virtual and pop-up exhibits. There is also the Art of Dying Institute, an initiative of the New York Open Center that has researchers, scholars and investors focusing on "the theme of death."

The Death Positive and Green Burial movements are unified in their break from the current death-care industry norms of extortionate and dispassionate conduct. The DIY approach can give friends and family the necessary time and space to part with the deceased in their own way. Putting one's affairs in order is an age-old way of easing the death burden. If a person's assets are straightforward, a last will and testament can be completed for free and without an attorney by filling in a template form with a list of assets, beneficiaries and an executor. Signatures from two witnesses are required, and the beneficiary and/or executor should then be informed of where that will is located. Additionally, planning one's own death ceremony and disposal method and making a record of it can prevent unnecessary costs. In the absence of a budget, making a list of preferences and a researched list of elected funeral service providers can minimize disagreements among the bereaved.

The dead and the dying are a ticking reminder of the inevitable, but in the city that never sleeps, the communities gathered by a lifetime will continue to search for the most felicitous version of the Good Death. In New York, secrets in the soil continue to be unearthed, just as new ideas, be they profitable, philosophical or practical, regarding where to put the dead and how best to memorialize them within the occupied space of a restless and determined city, are springing up in communities and research groups. There is a lot to consider: the ceremony, funerary fees, space selection, the distribution of wealth and debt, and ultimately, preparing for and adapting to the aftermath of a life lived.

BIBLIOGRAPHY

Books

Amanik, Allan. *Dust to Dust: A History of Jewish Death and Burial in New York.* New York: New York University Press, 2019.

Asbury, Herbert. *The Gangs of New York: An Informal History of the Underworld.* New York: Vintage, 2008.

Bailey, Harriet. *Nursing Mental Diseases.* New York: Macmillan, 1920.

Baxter, Albert. *History of the City of Grand Rapids, Michigan.* New York: Munsell and Company, 1891.

Bayles, Richard Mather. *History of Richmond County (Staten Island), New York: From Its Discovery to the Present Time, Part 1.* New York: L.E. Preston and Co., 1887.

Bolton, Robert. *A History of the County of Westchester, From Its First Settlement to the Present Time.* Vol. 1. New York: Alexander S. Gould, 1848.

Brown, Henry Collins. *Valentine's Manual of Old New York, No. 7, New Series.* New York: Valentine's Manual, 1923.

Bruck, Connie. *Master of the Game: How Steve Ross Rode the Light Fantastic from Undertaker to Creator of the Largest Media Conglomerate in the World.* New York: Simon and Schuster, 2013.

Burnett, John. *Minutes of Coroner's Proceedings: City and State of New York, John Burnet, Coroner, 174–1758.* Edited by Francis J. Sypher Jr. New York: New York Genealogical and Biographical Society, 2004.

Cohen, Patricia Cline. *The Murder of Helen Jewett: The Life and Death of a Prostitute in Nineteenth-Century New York.* New York: Vintage, 1998.

Comfort, Randall. *History of Bronx Borough, City of New York*. New York: North Side News Press, 1906.

Corporation Code. Laws of New York Relating to Private Corporations, Joint Stock Companies, and Associations, Including Suits and Proceedings by and against Them, and the Officers Thereof, in Civil and Criminal Actions and Proceedings. Edited by a member of the N.Y. Bar. New York: L.K. Strouse and Co., 1884.

Defoe, Daniel. *A Journal of the Plague Year (Norton Critical Edition)*. New York: W.W. Norton and Company, 1992.

Denton, Daniel. *A Brief Description of New York*. New York: WM. Van Norden, 1845.

Einstein, Isidor, and Stanley Walker. *Prohibition Agent No. 1*. New York: Frederick A. Stokes Company, 1932.

Faust, Drew Gilpin. *This Republic of Suffering: Death and the American Civil War*. New York: Vintage Books, 2009.

Fay, Theodore Sedgwick, ed. *The New York Mirror: A Weekly Gazette of Literature and the Fine Arts*. Vol. 8. New York: G.P. Morris, 1830.

Fernow, Berthold, ed. *The Records of New Amsterdam From 1653 to 1674 Anno Domini*. New York: Knickerbocker Press, 1897.

Harper, Kenn. *Minik: The New York Eskimo*. Hanover, NH: Steerforth Press, 2017.

Hastings, Hugh. *Ecclesiastical Records State of New York*. Vol. 2. Albany, NY: James B. Lyon, 1901.

Headley, Joel Tyler. *The Great Riots of New York, 1712 to 1873: Including a Full and Complete Account of the Four Days Draft Riot of 1863*. New York: E.B. Treat, 1873.

Griffin, Martin I.J., ed. *The American Catholic Historical Researches*. Vol. 18 Philadelphia: American Catholic Historical Society, 1901.

Ingham, George, PhD. *Irish Rebel, American Patriot: William James MacNeven, 1763–1841*. CreateSpace Independent Publishing Platform, 2014.

Inskeep, Carolee. *The Graveyard Shift: A Family Historian's Guide to New York City Cemeteries*. Orem, UT: Ancestry, 2000.

Judson, Selden C. *The Cemeteries of New York, and How to Reach Them*. New York: G.H. Burton, 1881.

King, Rufus. *The Life and Correspondence of Rufus King*. Edited by Charles R. King. New York: G.P. Putnam's Sons, 1898.

Kraft, Herbert C., and John T. Kraft. *The Indians of Lenapehoking*. South Orange, NJ: Seton Hall University Museum, 1988.

McAtamney, Hugh Entwistle. *Cradle Days of New York (1609–1835)*. New York: Drew and Lewis, 1909.

Minutes of the Common Council of the City of New York 1675–1776. New York: Dodd, Meade and Company, 1905.

Minutes of the Common Council of the City of New York 1784–1831. Vol. 1. New York: City of New York, 1917.

Minutes of the Common Council of the City of New York, 1784–1831. Vol. 15. New York: M.B. Brown, 1917.

Mitchell, Joseph. "Mr. Hunter's Grave." In *Up in the Old Hotel*, 504–36. New York: Vintage Books, 2008.

Mitford, Jessica. *The American Way of Death Revisited.* New York: Vintage Books, 2000.

Okrent, Daniel. *Great Fortune: The Epic of Rockefeller Center.* New York: Penguin, 2003.

Oppenheim, Samuel. *The Early History of the Jews in New York, 1654–1664: Some New Matter on the Subject.* Baltimore: Johns Hopkins University Press, originally published 1909.

Oshinsky, David. *Bellevue: Three Centuries of Medicine and Mayhem at America's Most Storied Hospital.* New York: Anchor Books, 2017.

Pasko, W.W., ed. *Old New York: A Journal Related to the History and Antiquities of New York City.* Vol. 1. New York: W.W. Pasko, 1890.

Peterson, Arthur Everett. *Landmarks of New York: A Guide to Historic Places.* New York: City History Club, 1924.

Peterson, Carla L. *Black Gotham: A Family History of African Americans in Nineteenth-Century New York City.* New Haven: Yale University Press, 2011.

Pliny the Elder. *The Natural History of Pliny.* Vol. 6. Translated by John Bostock (1773–1846) and Herny T. Riley (1816–1878). London: Henry G. Bohn, 1855.

Publications of the American Jewish Historical Society, 1909. Vol. 18 (Classic Reprint). London: Forgotten Books, 2017

Ruttenber, Edward Manning. *Footprints of the Red Men: Indian Geographical Names in the Valley of Hudson's River, the Valley of the Mohawk, and on the Delaware: Their Location and the Probable Meaning of Some of Them.* New York: New York State Historical Association, 1906.

Sarat, Austin. *Gruesome Spectacles: Botched Executions and America's Death Penalty.* Stanford, CA: Stanford University Press, 2014.

Shorto, Russell. *The Island at the Center of the World.* New York: Vintage Books, 2005.

Skinner, Alanson. *The Indians of Manhattan Island and Vicinity.* New York: American Museum of Natural History, 1921.

Smith, James McCune. *The Works of James McCune Smith: Black Intellectual and Abolitionist.* New York: Oxford University Press, 2007.

Tebb, William, and Edward Perry Vollum. *Premature Burial and How It May Be Prevented, with Special Reference to Trance, Catalepsy, and Other Forms of Suspended Animation.* London: Swan Sonnenschein and Company, Limited, 1905.

Theosophical Society. *The Theosophist.* Vol. 28. Edited by Helena Blavatsky. New York: Theosophical Publishing House, 1907.

Throop, Montgomery H., ed. *The Revised Statutes of the State of New York: Passed from the Year 1778 to February 1, 1889.* Vol. 3. New York: Banks and Brothers, Lawbook Publishers, 1889.

Valentine, David Thomas. *Manual of the Corporation of the City of New York for 1856.* New York: McSpedon and Baker, 1856.

———. *Manual of the Corporation of the City of New York for the Years 1844–5.* Classic Reprint Edition. London: Forgotten Books, 2017.

Veit, Richard F., and Mark Nonestied. *New Jersey Cemeteries and Tombstones: History in the Landscape.* New Brunswick, NJ: Rutgers University Press, 2008.

Weeks, Lyman Horace. *Prominent Families of New York: Being an Account in Biographical Form of Individuals and Families Distinguished as Representatives of the Social, Professional, and Civic Life of New York City.* New York: Historical Company, 1898.

White, Shane. *Prince of Darkness: The Untold Story of Jeremiah G. Hamilton, Wall Street's First Black Millionaire.* New York: Picador, 2016.

Wilson, Scott. *Resting Places: The Burial Sites of More Than 14,000 Famous Persons.* Jefferson, NC: McFarland, 2016.

Articles

Abbot, Karen. "Prohibitions Premier Hooch Hounds." *Smithsonian Magazine,* January 2012.

Ajamu, Amadi. "Celebration and Re-interment of Our Ancestors." *New York Amsterdam News,* August 1, 2019.

Aratani, Lauren. "Rats and Raw Sewage: Jeffrey Epstein Jail Blighted by 'Horrible' Conditions." *The Guardian.* August 17, 2019. https://www.theguardian.com/us-news/2019/aug/17/jeffrey-epstein-new-york-metropolitan-correctional-center-jail.

Associated Press. "Judy Garland's Remains Moved from New York to L.A." *Hollywood Reporter,* January 31, 2017. https://www.hollywoodreporter.com/lifestyle/lifestyle-news/judy-garlands-remains-moved-ny-la-970567/.

——— "Wisconsin: Cemetery Fund Not Protected From Creditors." *New York Times,* March 9, 2015.

The Associated Press and Raanan Geberer. "Green-Wood Cemetery Reburies 200-Year-Old Bodies under Washington Square Park." *Brooklyn Daily Eagle*, March 2, 2021.

Barnes, Mike. "John 'Cha Cha' Ciarcia, Actor on 'The Sopranos,' Dies at 69." *Hollywood Reporter*. December 1, 2015. https://www.hollywoodreporter.com/tv/tv-news/john-ciarcia-dead-sopranos-actor-844917/.

Barron, James. "Baden Dismissal Ordered for Comment in Article about Murder." *New York Times*. December 22, 1982.

———— "Koch Dismisses Gross, Faulting His Leadership." *New York Times*, October 30, 1987.

Bascome, Erik. "Staten Island's Mount Richmond Cemetery: A Struggle to Keep Up with Coronavirus Burials." silive.com. Updated April 21, 2020. https://www.silive.com/news/j66j-2020/04/c2466db3223676/staten-islands-mount-richmond-cemetery-a-struggle-to-keep-up-with-coronavirus-burials.html.

Baugher, Sherene, and Edward J. Lenik. "Anatomy of an Almshouse Complex." *Northeast Historical Archaeology* 26, article 2 (1997). DOI: 10.22191/neha/vol26/iss1/2.

BBC News. "Greek Woman 'Buried Alive by Accident.'" September 26, 2014. https://www.bbc.com/news/world-europe-29373806.

Benincasa, Robert. "You Could Pay Thousands Less for a Funeral Just by Crossing the Street." NPR. February 7, 2017. https://www.npr.org/2017/02/07/504020003/a-funeral-may-cost-you-thousands-less-just-by-crossing-the-street.

Benner, Katie, et al. "Before Jail Suicide, Jeffrey Epstein Was Left Alone and Not Closely Monitored." *New York Times*, August 11, 2019.

Benton, Ned. "Dating the Start and End of Slavery in New York." CUNY Academic Commons, Slavery Records Index. https://nyslavery.commons.gc.cuny.edu/dating-the-start-and-end-of-slavery-in-new-york/.

Bernstein, Nina. "Bill Would Require Relatives' Consent for Schools to Use Cadavers." *New York Times*, June 26, 2016.

———— "New York State Bans Use of Unclaimed Dead as Cadavers Without Consent." *New York Times*, August 19, 2016

———— "Unearthing the Secrets of New York's Mass Graves." *New York Times*, May 15, 2016.

Beschloss, Michael. "When T.R. Saw Lincoln." *New York Times*, May 21, 2014.

Besonen, Julie. "Resting Place for the High and the Low." *New York Times*, February 6, 2015.

Biederman, Marcia. "Neighborhood Report: Prospect Park/Park Slope; He's Here for Eternity, but Don't Ask Where." *New York Times*, September 27, 1998.

Blumenthal, Ralph. "A Man Who Knew About the Electric Chair." *New York Times*, November 6, 2011.

Bone, James. "Undertaker Admits Stealing and Selling Alistair Cooke Body Parts." *The Times*, October 20, 2006. https://www.thetimes.co.uk/article/undertaker-admits-stealing-and-selling-alistair-cooke-body-parts-x7pj0z6f29h.

Brent, Harry. "The Incredible Story of 'Durable' Mike Molloy—A Donegal Man Living in New York Who Simply Refused to Die." *Irish Post*, July 29, 2019. https://www.irishpost.com/life-style/incredible-story-durable-mike-malloy-donegal-man-living-new-york-simply-refused-die-169395.

Brooklyn Daily Eagle. "Blind Tom Is An Issue: Did He Die At Johnstown?" December 27, 1903.

———. "Favour Greater Use of Typhoid Serum." September 5, 1915.

———. "An Old Farmer's Talk. Stephen L. Vanderveer's New Lots Recollections." September 19, 1886.

Brown, Patricia Leigh. "A Passion for Graveyard Art that Took a Criminal Turn; Tiffany Glass and Other Tales From the Crypt." *New York Times*, September 5, 1999.

Bryce, Robert. "Final Disposition." *Austin (TX) Chronicle.* May 14, 2004.

——— "Funeralgate Hits Texas. What Did Bush Know?" *Austin (TX) Chronicle.* July 9, 1999.

Buffalo Evening News. "Lemuel Smith's Dead." August 11, 1881.

Buffalo Morning Express. "Hiram Cronk at 105." March 7, 1905.

Butler, Eoin. "The Cork Girl Who Was First through Ellis Island's Gates." *Irish Times*, February 3, 2017. https://www.irishtimes.com/life-and-style/abroad/the-cork-girl-who-was-first-through-ellis-island-s-gates-1.2958208.

Calver, William. "Recollections of Northern Manhattan." *NYHS* 32, no. 1 (January 1948). New York Historical Society Digital Archives. https://digitalcollections.nyhistory.org/islandora/object/islandora%3A13852#page/1/mode/1up.

Canedy, Dana. "Funeral Company Manager, Upset by Suit, Is Found Dead." *New York Times*, December 29, 2001.

Chaudry, Aliya. "Ongoing Struggle to Get Recognition for Slave Burial Ground at Joseph Rodman Drake Park." *Bronx Ink*, 2018. http://bronxink.org/parks-2018/ongoing-struggle-to-get-recognition-for-slave-burial-ground-at-joseph-rodman-drake-park/.

Clines, Francis X. "About New York." *New York Times*, May 10, 1977.

Cobb, Geoffrey. "Kelly Was True Renaissance Man." *Irish Echo*, May 19, 2020. https://www.irishecho.com/2020/05/kelly-was-true-renaissance-man/.

Cohen, Jason. "Park Honors Enslaved African Burial Ground with New Signs in Joseph Rodman Drake Park." *Bronx Times*, January 27, 2021. https://www.bxtimes.com/parks-honors-enslaved-african-burial-ground-with-new-signs-in-joseph-rodman-drake-park/.

Connolly, Father Sean. "The Age of Miracles Has Not Passed." *Catholic World Report*, November 12, 2019. https://www.catholicworldreport.com/2019/11/12/the-age-of-miracles-has-not-passed/.

Cooney, Betty M. "Black Magic Suspected in Theft of Cypress Hills Corpse." *Queens Chronicle*, August 17, 2000. https://www.qchron.com/editions/central/black-magic-suspected-in-theft-of-cypress-hills-corpse/article_562e59f8-6aa1-55c8-880f-aeb75dc37294.html.

Cormier, Amanda. "Graves' End." *BKLYNR*, April 18, 2013. https://www.bklynr.com/graves-end/.

Davis, Feather Ann. "Medicare Hospice Benefit: Early Program Experiences." *Healthcare Financing Review*, 9, no. 4 (Summer 1988). https://www.cms.gov/research-statistics-data-and-systems/research/healthcarefinancingreview/downloads/cms1192048dl.pdf.

Davis, Thomas J. "These Enemies of Their Own Household: Slaves in 18th Century New York." In *A Beautiful and Fruitful Place: Selected Rensselaerswijck Seminar Papers*, vol. 1. Edited by Nancy Anne McClure Zeller. Albany, NY: New Netherland Publishing, 1991. https://www.newnetherlandinstitute.org/programs/events/new-netherland-seminar/a-beautiful-and-fruitful-place/.

DePalma, Anthony. "City Says Prescription Misuse Caused Death of Detective Who Worked at 9/11 Site." *New York Times*, October 26, 2007.

Duggan, Paul. "Bush Need Not Testify, Judge Rules Bush Need Not Testify, Judge Rules." *Washington Post*, August 31, 1999.

Dunlap, David W. "New Life for Staten Island's Derelict Farm Colony." *New York Times*, January 20, 2016.

Dunn, Ashley. "A Heritage Reclaimed: From Old Artifacts, American Indians Shape a New Museum." *New York Times*, October 9, 1994.

Easum, Donald. "Wanted: Tenants for 'Ghost' Isles." *New York Times*, August 24, 1949.

Edelman, Susan. "The Mortician School Cheating Scandal That Could Ruin City Funeral Homes." *New York Post*, March 10, 2018.

Evans, Laura. "Oopsy: Ed Koch's Tombstone Has Glaring Typo." *Gothamist*, June 18, 2013. https://gothamist.com/news/oopsy-ed-kochs-tombstone-has-glaring-typo.

Evening Post. "Burying Ground: The Common Council at Their Last Sitting." June 12, 1823.

———. "To Elisha W. King, Esq." November 20, 1823.

Fahey, Ryan. "Woman Spots Her 'Dead' Mother, 89, Is ALIVE Just Seconds before She Was CREMATED." *Daily Mail*, January 27, 2021. https://www.dailymail.co.uk/news/article-9193123/Woman-spots-dead-mother-89-ALIVE-just-seconds-CREMATED.html.

Feuer, Alan. "Dentist Pleads Guilty to Stealing and Selling Body Parts." *New York Times*, March 19, 2008.

——— "Ronell Wilson, Killer of 2 Detectives, Will Not Face Death Penalty." *New York Times*, March 15, 1016.

Franz, Bill. "Memorial to Martyred Mariners Rededicated [excerpts from *Newark Star-Ledger*]." *American Merchant Marine at War*, August 26, 1997. http://www.usmm.org/martyrs.html.

Gallagher, Thomas. "American Heritage Book Selection: The Body Snatchers." *American Heritage* 18, no. 4 (1967). https://www.americanheritage.com/american-heritage-book-selection-body-snatchers.

Goodstein, Laurie. "Dolan Sought to Protect Church Assets, Files Show." *New York Times*, July 1, 2013.

Gray, Christopher. "Streetscapes: The Elks Club; An Endangered Species on 43d." *New York Times*, December 13, 1987.

———. "Streetscapes/150th Street and St. Nicholas Place; 1888 Mansion Built by the Bailey of Barnum & Bailey." *New York Times.* April 8, 2001.

Greenberg, Erik J. "City Blasts Funeral Home Giant." *New York Jewish Week*, February 12, 1999. https://jewishweek.timesofisrael.com/city-blasts-funeral-home-giant/.

Griffin, Allie. "Board Members of Non-Profit Cemetery Embezzled Thousands of Dollars." *Ridgewood Post*, September 4, 2019. https://ridgewoodpost.com/board-members-of-non-profit-cemetery-embezzled-thousands-of-dollars.

Gross, Charles. "The Early History and Influence of the Officer of Coroner." *Political Science Quarterly* 7, no. 4 (December 1892): 656–72. https://www.jstor.org/stable/pdf/2139446.pdf.

Gross, Jane. "Quiet Doctor Finds a Mission in Assisted Suicide Court Case." *New York Times*, January 2, 1997.

Haberman, Clyde. "An Affront to the Dead, and the Living." *New York Times*, June 13, 1997.

Hacker, J. David. "A Census-Based Count of the Civil War Dead." Civil War History 57, no. 4 (2011): 307–48. DOI:10.1353/cwh.2011.0061.

Hearth, Amy Hill. "The Bones of Indians, but Not the Chief." *New York Times*, March 26, 1989

Herrera, Kevin. "Police Say Suspect Sliced Off Another's Ear Over Unpaid Debt." *Santa Monica Daily Press*, April 20, 2012. https://www.smdp.com/police-say-suspect-sliced-off-anothers-ear-over-unpaid-debt/80612.

Heydarpour, Roja. "At Muslim Resting Place, 5 New Child-Size Graves." *New York Times*, March 18, 2007.

Hickey, Kate. "Burying the Irish Famine Dead in Staten Island." *Irish Central*, June 27, 2017. https://www.irishcentral.com/roots/history/burying-irish-famine-dead-staten-island.

Honan, William H. "Paderewski's Remains to Return to Poland." *New York Times*, November 12, 1990.

Hosack, David. "To the Right Revd. Bishop Hobart." *Evening Post* (New York, NY), June 5, 1823.

Hu, Winnie. "Learning to Speak for the Dead." *New York Times*, June 10, 2016.

Im, Jimmy. "People Stopped Booking the Trump Soho Hotel Postelection, So It Rebranded—Take a Look Inside." CNBC. Updated June 8, 2018. https://www.cnbc.com/2018/06/08/photos-trump-soho-now-the-dominick-hotel-in-new-york-city.html.

Jewish Post. "N.Y. Jewish Community Buys $2.7 Million Funeral Chapel." https://www.jewishpost.com/archives/news/ny-jewish-community-buys-2-million-funeral-chapel.html.

Katinas, Paula. "Report: Body Snatching Doctor Is Dying of Bone Cancer." *Brooklyn Daily Eagle*, April 1, 2013. https://brooklyneagle.com/articles/2013/04/01/report-body-snatching-doctor-is-dying-of-bone-cancer/.

Kearney, Kevin. "Son of Sam Investigator Reflects on 40th Anniversary." *Tri-County Independent*, August 5, 2016. https://www.tricountyindependent.com/news/20160805/son-of-sam-investigator-reflects-on-40th-anniversary.

Kihss, Peter. "500 Gravestones in Queens Toppled in Latest Outbreak." *New York Times*, March 28, 1979.

Kilgannon, Corey. "Dead of AIDS and Forgotten in Potter's Field." *New York Times*, July 3, 2018.

Knapman, Paul. "The Crowner's Quest." *Journal of the Royal Society of Medicine* 86 (December 1993). http://europepmc.org/backend/ptpmcrender.fcgi?accid=PMC1294365&blobtype=pdf.

Kurutz, Stephen. "Neighborhood Report: Chinatown; The Street of No Return." *New York Times*, August 29, 2004.

Leduff, Charlie. "3 Cemeteries Are Haunted By Vandals." *New York Times*, November 24, 1996.

Lee, Stephen. "Round-the-Clock Cremations Stoke Mercury Fears for Neighborhoods." *Bloomberg Law*, May 15, 2020. https://news.bloomberglaw.com/environment-and-energy/round-the-clock-cremations-stoke-mercury-fears-for-neighborhoods

Lewin, Tamar. "Funeral Company Accused of Desecration." *New York Times*, December 21, 2001.

Lumer, Michael, and Nancy Tenney. "The Death Penalty in New York: An Historical Perspective." *Journal of Law and Policy* 4, no. 1, art. 5 (1995). https://brooklynworks.brooklaw.edu/cgi/viewcontent.cgi?article=1461&context=jlp.

Martin, Douglass. "After Benny Ong, Silence in Chinatown." *New York Times*, August 8, 1994.

Montgomery, Paul L. "Skeletons Found in Washington Sq.; 25 Uncovered in a Sealed Room at Con Ed Project." *New York Times*, August 2, 1965.

Moynihan, Colin. "A Quest to Recognize Forgotten Achievements Still Relevant in Everyday Life." *New York Times*, May 26, 2014.

Nathan-Kazis, Josh. "Black Market for Jewish Grave Sites Grows on Web." *Forward*, February 14, 2013. https://forward.com/news/171161/black-market-for-jewish-grave-sites-grows-on-web/?p=all.

News and Herald (Winnsboro, SC). "A Ghastly Ceremony." 1876.

New York Daily Herald. "The New York Crystal Palace. Public Proposal for Its Removal." June 3, 1856.

New York Times. "Anton Seidl's Funeral; Public Memorial Demonstration Held at the Metropolitan Opera House. Thousands in Attendance. The Address Delivered by the Rev. Merle St. Croix Wright and a Telegram Sent by Robert G. Ingersoll—The Body Cremated." April 1, 1898.

———. "The Blind Tom Mystery." June 18, 1908.

———. "Dr. Charles De Costa Brown." July 14, 1896.

———. "Empty Graves in Trinity Cemetery; Removal of the Bodies There Discloses Strange Carelessness of Former Workmen." April 14, 1911.

———. "Execution of Hicks, the Pirate; Twelve Thousand People at Bedloe's Island. Scenes at the Tombs, in the Bay, and at the Place of Execution. His Confession." July 14, 1860.

———. "Far Worse than Hanging. Kemmler's Death Proves an Awful Spectacle. The Electric Current Had to Be Turned On Twice before the Deed Was Fully Accomplished." August 7, 1890.

———. "The Ghastly Ceremony of Incinerating the Remains." *New York Times*, December 7, 1876.

———. "Hans Schimdt Dies Today; Ex-Priest Says He Is Going to His Death Because He Lied." February 18, 1916.

———. "In the Crematory Fires: The First Body in the Retort at Mount Olivet. Friends, Relatives, and Other Interested Persons Watch the First Incineration of Eugene Lievre." December 5, 1885.

———. "The Last Electrocution." March 7, 1995.

———. "The Last Hanging: There Was a Reason They Outlawed Public Execution." May 6, 2001.

———. "Little Italy Mourns Il Gran 'Bacigalup'; Undertaker Who Has Buried 1,000 at His Own Expense Awaits the Tomb. Began as a Bootblack, Rose to Affluence and Never Let One of the Colony's Penniless Dead Go to Potter's Field." December 1, 1908.

———. "Manhattan Yields Mastodon's Bones; Workmen Dig Up Remains of the Island's Oldest Known Inhabitant at Inwood. Lived 10,000 Years Ago. Fossils Presented to the American Museum—Souvenir Hunters Steal 13 of 14 Huge Teeth." March 26, 1925.

———. "Montgomery Clift Dead at 45; Nominated 3 Times for Oscar; Completed Last Movie, 'The Defector,' in June Actor Began Career at Age 13." July 24, 1966.

———. "Mrs. Halliday, Insane, Stabs Nurse 200 Times; Locks Her in Matteawan Room and Kills Her with Scissors. Resented Her Departure. She Had Threatened to Kill Miss Wickes If the Latter Left the State Hospital." September 28, 1906.

———. "The Obsequies." April 26, 1865.

———. "Petrosino Slain Assassins Gone; New York Detective, While Tracking Sicilian Criminals, Shot in Palermo Square." March 14, 1909.

———. "The Political Murder; Trial of Richard Croker for Killing John McKenna." *New York Times*, December 11, 1874.

———. "President Scores Virus of Bigotry." January 13, 1960.

———. "The Quarantine Conflagration." September 4, 1858.

———. "The Result Yesterday—Large Registration of Colored Voters." May 14, 1870.

———. "Shaaray Tefila Jubilee: The Congregation a Vigorous Child of B'nai Jeshurun." *New York Times*, March 21, 1896.

———. "Skeletons in the War; Bones and Coffins Unearthed in Washington Square." May 13, 1890.

———. "Slayer of Budd Girl Dies in Electric Chair; Albert Fish, 65, Pays Penalty at Sing-Sing—Bronx Negro Also Is Put to Death." January 17, 1936.

———. "Stabbed to Death in Office Frolic." February 16, 1909.

———. "Trinity Improvements: A New Parish School-House and a New Iron Suspension Bridge Expenditure of $112,000. The New Building. The Suspension Bridge." June 15, 1871.

———. "Unearth Skeleton in Park; But Plumbers Learn That Madison Square Once Was Potter's Field." September 11, 1930.

New York Tribune. "Not a Shot Fired as Tong Escorts Ko Low to Grave." August 14, 1922.

———. "Public Health—Potter's Field Again." April 7, 1857.

Owensboro (KY) Messenger. "Hanged Negro Is Buried 3 Hours after Execution." August 15, 1936.

Paybarah, Azi. "Epstein's Autopsy 'Points to Homicide,' Pathologist Hired by Brother Claims." *New York Times.* Updated October 31, 2019. https://www.nytimes.com/2019/10/30/nyregion/jeffrey-epstein-homicide-autopsy-michael-baden.html.

Pehek, Ellen. "Salamander Diversity and Distribution in New York City 1820 to the Present." *Transactions of the Linnaen Society of New York* 10 (2007): 157-83. https://www.academia.edu/933744/Salamander_Diversity_and_Distribution_in_New_York_City_1820_to_the_Present.

Pengelly, Martin. "Families of 9/11 Victims Protest Against Move of Remains to New York Museum." *The Guardian*, May 10, 2014. https://www.theguardian.com/world/2014/may/10/911-victims-families-protest-move-remains-new-york-museum.

Petri, Alexandra E. "The Mortuary Science Professor Who Came 'Out of Nowhere' to Help NYC." *New York Times*, April 22, 2020.

Pollack, Michael. "Who Was the Real Ichabod Crane?" *New York Times*, October 16, 2015.

Rasenberger, Jim. "City Lore; 'The Witch of Staten Island.'" *New York Times*, October 29, 2000.

"Return to the African Burial Ground: An Interview with Physical Anthropologist Michael L. Blakey." *Archaeology*, November 20, 2003. https://archive.archaeology.org/online/interviews/blakey/.

Rice, Lynette. "Oscars Flashback: The Tragic Life and Death of Former Disney Star Bobby Driscoll." *Entertainment Weekly.* January 22, 2019. https://ew.com/oscars/2019/01/22/bobby-driscoll-former-disney-star-oscar-winner/.

Richmond, Caroline. "Dame Cicely Saunders." US National Library of Medicine. July 23, 2005. https://www.ncbi.nlm.nih.gov/pmc/articles/PMC1179787/.

Rivera, Ray, and Andy Newman. "Explosives Abandoned in Cemetery Are Mystery." *New York Times*, October 11, 2010.

Roberts, Sam. "Honoring a Very Early New Yorker." *New York Times*, October 2, 2012. https://cityroom.blogs.nytimes.com/2012/10/02/honoring-a-very-early-new-yorker/.

————. "Koch, Resolved to Spend Eternity in Manhattan, Buys a Cemetery Plot." *New York Times*, April 22, 2008.

Rogers, Rosemary. "Wild Irish Women: 'Hello Suckers!'" *Irish America Magazine*, April–May 2018. https://www.irishamerica.com/2018/02/wild-irish-women-hello-suckers/.

Rohde, David. "A Store Owner Pleads Guilty to Transporting Fetuses Illegally." *New York Times*, March 27, 1998.

———— "Expert Guilty in Scheme to Steal Tiffany Glass from Tombs." *New York Times*, April 13, 1999.

Rosa, Jerry, and Dick Sheridan. "Heads-Up Cops Bag Suspect." *Daily News*, July 18, 1991.

Rueb, Emily S. "When Important People Die, He's There." *New York Times*, May 15, 2019.

Santora, Marc. "City Cemeteries Face Gridlock." *New York Times*, August 13, 2010.

Saul, Josh. "Family of Mistakenly Cremated Buddhist: 'She's Doomed to Eternal Shame.'" *New York Post*, September 11, 2014.

Seeman, Erik R. "Reassessing the 'Sankofa Symbol' in New York's African Burial Ground." *William and Mary Quarterly* 67, no. 1 (2010): 101–22. https://www.jstor.org/stable/10.5309/willmaryquar.67.1.101.

Severo, Richard. "Koch Removes Baden as the City's Medical Examiner." *New York Times*, August 1, 1979.

Sheehan, Kevin, and Philip Messing. "Ex-'Storage Wars' Buyer Wins Locker Full of Human Ashes." *New York Post*, February 11, 2015.

Shipp, E.R. "Black Cemetery Yields Wealth of History." *New York Times*, August 9, 1992.

Singer, Jeffrey, and Corey Kilgannon. "Yes, He Sold Fakes. They Are Supposed to Be Fake." *New York Times*, August 24, 2011.

Stack, Liam. "'Plague on a Biblical Scale': Hasidic Families Hit Hard by Virus." *New York Times*, April 21, 2020.

Stillman, John. "For $350K You Can Spend Eternity in Manhattan." *Gothamist.* Updated October 23, 2015. https://gothamist.com/news/for-350k-you-can-spend-eternity-in-manhattan.

Strom, Stephanie. "Same Burial, Minus the Markup; Nonprofit Funeral Home Gains Fans by Cutting Costs." *New York Times*, August 7, 2003.

The Sun (New York, NY). "Hiram Cronk Lies in State." May 18, 1895.

———. "Whole City Honors Hiram Cronk, Last Survivor of War of 1812." March 18, 1895.

Surico, John. "How Do Psychics Survive in New York City?" *Vice.* March 11, 2015. https://www.vice.com/en/article/yvqyab/how-do-psychics-survive-in-new-york-city-311.

Syme, Rachel. "Dawn Powell's Masterful Gossip: Why Won't It Sell?" *The New Yorker*, July 23, 2012.

Thompson, Cole. "Inwood's Forgotten Slave Cemetery." My Inwood. November 17, 2015. https://myinwood.net/inwoods-forgotten-slave-cemetery/#:~:text=In%20March%20of%201903%20workmen,buried%20beneath%20crude%20stone%20markers.

Vick, Karl. "An Execution in the Old Way." *Washington Post*, January 26, 1996.

Vitello, Paul. "With Demise of Jewish Burial Societies, Resting Places Are in Turmoil." *New York Times*, August 2, 2009.

Waller, Allyson, and Derrick Bryson Taylor. "They Thought She Was Dead. Then She Woke Up at a Funeral Home." *New York Times.* Updated October 19, 2020. https://www.nytimes.com/2020/08/25/us/michigan-woman-alive-funeral-home.html.

Weir, Richard. "Neighborhood Report: East Harlem; Start-Off for a Final Journey." *New York Times*, February 21, 1999.

White, E.B., and Ivan Sandrof. "The First Embalmer." *The New Yorker*, October 30, 1942.

White, Josh. "Funeral Home Employees Say Bodies Were Mishandled." *Washington Post*, April 5, 2009.

——— "Funeral Home Firm Service Corporation International Faces Lawsuits, Complaints." *Washington Post*, April 26, 2009.

Wilson, Michael. "Telling Fortunes, and, from Time to Time, Also Taking Them." *New York Times*, August 5, 2011.

Yuhas, Alan. "Two Centuries-Old Tombs Unearthed beneath Historic New York City Park." *The Guardian*, November 7, 2015. https://www.theguardian.com/us-news/2015/nov/07/new-york-city-burial-vaults-washington-square-park.

Documents, Records and Reports

"A.G. Schneiderman Announces Indictment of Attorney for Stealing Nearly $2 Million." New York State Office of the Attorney General Press Release Archives. February 10, 2014. https://ag.ny.gov/press-release/2014/ag-schneiderman-announces-indictment-attorney-stealing-nearly-2-million.

Adams, Bradley J., MD, and Christian M Crowder, MD. "Report of Findings: Archaeological Investigation of the Spring Street Presbyterian Church Cemetery." Office of the Chief Medical Examiner of the City of New York. 2008. http://s-media.nyc.gov/agencies/lpc/arch_reports/1139.pdf.

"An Act for the Punishment of Certain Crimes Against the United States." First Congress of the United States, Session 2, Ch. 8, 9. 1790.

"Annual Reports of the Bureau of Military Statistics." New York State Military Museum and Veterans Research Center. 1864–68. https://museum.dmna.ny.gov/unit-history/conflict/us-civil-war-1861-1865/annual-reports-bureau-military-statistics.

"The Archeology of 290 Broadway Volume 1 and 2: The Secular Use of Lower Manhattan's African Burial Ground." Compiled and edited by Charles D. Cheek, PhD, and Daniel G. Roberts, RPA. New York: John Milner Associates Inc., 2009. https://www.nps.gov/afbg/learn/historyculture/upload/Volume_I_290Broadway.pdf.

"Attorney General Becerra Files Unlawful Business Practices against Neptune Society, Company Offering Prepaid Cremation Service (Press Release)." State of California Department of Justice, Office of the Attorney General. December 2, 2019. https://oag.ca.gov/news/press-releases/attorney-general-becerra-files-unlawful-business-practices-action-against.

Baldwin, Geraldine E., et al. "Van Cortlandt Park Parade Ground Phase 1A Archeological Investigation." Croton on Hudson, NY: John Millner Associates Inc, 2007. http://s-media.nyc.gov/agencies/lpc/arch_reports/1029.pdf.

Blakely, Michael L., et al. *The New York African Burial Ground*: *Unearthing the African Presence in Colonial New York*. 3 vols. Washington, D.C.: Howard University Press, 2009. https://www.nps.gov/afbg/learn/historyculture/upload/Vol-5-Gen-Aud-NYABG-DOWN.pdf.

Bucklew v. Precythe, Director, Missouri Department of Corrections, et al. Supreme Court of the United States. Argued November 6, 2018, Decided April 1, 2019. (No. 17-8151).

"Chapter 4—Decisions at Life's End: Existing Law." New York State Department of Health. https://www.health.ny.gov/regulations/task_force/reports_publications/when_death_is_sought/chap4.htm.

Commonwealth of Pennsylvania v. Michael Mastromarino. No. 3443 EDA 2008. Decided July 21, 2010. Superior Court of Pennsylvania.

Cuomo, Andrew, Governor. "Executive Order, no. 171: Organ Donation Policy." State of New York. October 16, 2017.

Dennis C. Vacco, Attorney General of New York, et al., Petitioners v. Timothy E. Quill, et al. United States Supreme Court. Decided June 26, 1997. (No. 95-1858).

Department of Veteran's Affairs. "America's Wars (Factsheet)." https://www.va.gov/opa/publications/factsheets/fs_americas_wars.pdf.

"Designation List 187, LP-1512, Former New York Life Insurance Building." Landmarks Preservation Commission. February 10, 1987. http://s-media.nyc.gov/agencies/lpc/lp/1512.pdf.

Dickinson, Nancy, and Faline Schneiderman-Fox. "St. Philip's Episcopal Church Cemetery Intensive Documentary Study, Chrystie Street, New York, New York, Second Avenue Subway." Historical Perspectives Inc. June 2003. http://s-media.nyc.gov/agencies/lpc/arch_reports/437.pdf.

Ellis, Meredith Alyson Berman. "Children of Spring Street: The Remains of Childhood in a Nineteenth Century Abolitionist Congregation." PhD diss., Syracuse University, 2014. https://surface.syr.edu/etd/48/.

Federal Trade Commission. "The FTC Funeral Rule." July 2012. https://www.consumer.ftc.gov/articles/0300-ftc-funeral-rule.

Funeral Consumers Alliance. "Response to Federal Trade Commission Request for Comments re: Funeral Industry Practices Rule 16 CFR Part 453." June 2020. https://funerals.org/wp-content/uploads/2020/06/2020-June-FCA-Final-Submission-to-FTC-Funeral-Rule-Review.pdf.

Geiger, Lisa, Alyssa Loorya, and Carol S. Weed. "Phase IA/IB Archaeological Assessment, NYC Farm Colony." White Plains: VHB Engineering, Surveying and Landscape Architecture, PC, 2014. http://s-media.nyc.gov/agencies/lpc/arch_reports/1627.pdf.

Hamilton, Alexander. "Petition to the Mayor, Aldermen, and Commonality of the State of New York [24 April 1797]." Founders Online. National Archives. https://founders.archives.gov/documents/Hamilton/01-21-02-0030.

Heaton, Patrick J. "Phase 1B Archaeological Investigation: Block 457, Lot 28 (Former Methodist Episcopal Cemetery) New York, New York." Croton on Hudson, NY: John Milner Associates Inc., 2005. http://s-media.nyc.gov/agencies/lpc/arch_reports/883.pdf.

Heaton, Patrick J., and Joel I. Klein. "Archaeological Investigations on Block 427, Lot 30 within the Cooper Square Urban Renewal Area." Croton on Hudson, NY: John Milner Associates, Inc., 2003. http://s-media.nyc.gov/agencies/lpc/arch_reports/450.pdf.

Hobson, Amos Herbert. 1888. Process of Separating Gelatine from Bones. U.S. Patent 39482A filed April 5, 1888, and issued December 25, 1888.

Howson, Jean, Leonard G. Bianchi and Warren R. Perry. "New York African Burial Ground Archaeology Final Report Volume 1 and 2." Washington, D.C.: Howard University, 2006. https://core.tdar.org/document/5716/new-york-african-burial-ground-archaeology-final-report-volume-1-archaeological-site-plan-map-figure-17.

Hurley, Marianne. "Designation List 487, LP-1233: FORT HAMILTON PARKWAY ENTRANCE Built 1876–77; Architect Richard Mitchell Upjohn. GREEN-WOOD CEMETERY CHAPEL. Built 1911–13; Architects Warren & Wetmore." Landmarks Preservation Commission. 2016. http://s-media.nyc.gov/agencies/lpc/lp/1233.pdf.

Jersey State Memorial Park v. Joseph Carlino, et al./The Mansuri Family v. Jersey State Memorial Park. Dockett No. C-185-15. Superior Court of New Jersey, Monmouth County, Chancery Division. http://www.jerseystatememorial.com/home/wp-content/uploads/2017/05/3.-Judgement-by-Judge-Cleary-04-26-2017.pdf.

Kearns, Betsy, and Cece Kirkorian. "Archaeological Impact Report for Bryant Park Restoration Corporation." Historical Perspectives Inc., 1983. http://s-media.nyc.gov/agencies/lpc/arch_reports/384.pdf.

Loorya, Alyssa, et al. "City Hall Rehabilitation Project 2010-2011." Edited by Alyssa Loorya and Christopher Ricciardi. Brooklyn: Chrysalis Archaeology; Burlington: URS Corporation, 2013. http://s-media.nyc.gov/agencies/lpc/arch_reports/1555.pdf.

MacLean, Jessica S., Lawrence B. Conyers and Shayleen M. Ottman. "Hunts Point Burial Ground, Drake Park, Bronx, New York: Phase 1A Documentary Study and Ground Penetrating Radar Survey." New York City Department of Parks and Recreation and New York Department of Education. 2017.

"Manumission of Manuel De Gerrit and Nine Other Negroes from Slavery, 25 February 1644" from *Van Laer, Council Minutes, Volume IV, 1638–1649*, doc. 183, pgs. 212–13. Translated by New Netherland Institute. https://www.newnetherlandinstitute.org/history-and-heritage/digital-exhibitions/slavery-exhibit/half-freedom/manumission-of-manuel-de-gerrit-and-nine-other-negroes-from-slavery/.

Mcknight, Walter J. Electric Device for Indicating the Awakening of Persons Buried Alive. U.S. Patent 652,934 filed May 20, 1899, and issued July 3, 1900.

"Medical Testimony before Richard Croker, Coroner, September 2, 1875." New York City Municipal Archives. National Library of Medicine online. Last updated June 6, 2014. https://www.nlm.nih.gov/exhibition/visibleproofs/galleries/exhibition/rise_image_12.html.

"Memorandum: 235 Bowery Street, Block 426/Lot 12, Manhattan Archaeological Field Investigation." Historical Perspectives Inc. April 9, 2006. http://s-media.nyc.gov/agencies/lpc/arch_reports/909.pdf.

"Military Affairs in New York 1861–1865." New York State Military Museum and Veterans Research Center. https://museum.dmna.ny.gov/unit-history/conflict/us-civil-war-1861-1865/military-affairs-new-york-1861-1865.

Muñiz, Edwin. "Geophysical Study Using Ground Penetrating Radar; Van Cortlandt Park; Old Putnam Trail; Bronx, NY." United States Department of Agriculture, 2019. https://kingsbridgehistoricalsociety.org/gprReport.pdf.

New York Assembly Bill A8883. For the Purposes of the Disposition of Human Remains, Includes Treatment of Such Remains by the Process of Alkaline Hydrolysis within the Definition of "Cremation." New York State Senate, 2011–12 Legislative Session. Active.

New York Assembly Bill 8883. Authorizes the Use of Alkaline Hydrolysis Tissue Digestion Process for the Disposal of Cadavers and Human Tissue Used for Medical Education. 2011–12 Legislative Session. Dead January 4, 2012.

New York City Farm Colony-Seaview Hospital Historic District Designation Report. Prepared by Shirley Zavin, Edited by Marjorie Pearson. New York: Landmark Preservation Commission, 1985. http://www.neighborhoodpreservationcenter.org/db/bb_files/1985NYCFarmColonySeaviewHospHistoricDistrict.pdf.

New York Consolidated Laws, Not-For-Profit Corporation Law - NPC § 1506. Cemetery Lands.

New York Health Code Article 205 Death and Disposals of Human Remains.

New York Penal Law § 165.35 Fortune Telling.

Obituary for Auguste Renouard (Aged 73). *Brooklyn Daily Eagle.* March 14, 1912.

Obituary for Dr. Thomas Holmes. *Brooklyn Daily Eagle.* January 10, 1900.

The People of the State of New York, by Letitia James, Attorney General of the State of New York, Plaintiff, v. Daniel C. Austin, Sr., Daniel C. Austin, Jr., Donald M. Pfail, Joseph Lodato, Michael W. Michel, Anthony R. Mordente, and Vera Princiotta, Defendants. People v. Austin, Index No. 451533/2019, (N.Y. Sup. Ct. 2021).

The People of the State of New York, Respondent v. Stephen S. LaValle, Appellant. New York State Court of Appeals. Argued April 26, 2004, Decided June 24, 2004. (3 NY3d at 99).

"Phase1 Cultural Resource Survey of Wayanda Park, Queens Village, Queens, Queens County, New York." Prepared by Alyssa Loorya and

Christopher Ricciardi. Landmarks Preservation Commission, 2003. http://s-media.nyc.gov/agencies/lpc/arch_reports/601.pdf.

Presa, Donald G. "Designation List 318, LP-2067: New York Life Insurance Company Building." Landmarks Preservation Commission. October 24, 2000. http://s-media.nyc.gov/agencies/lpc/lp/2067.pdf.

"Prospectus—Alteration, Ted Weiss Federal Building, New York, NY." Prospectus No. PNY-0350-NY15, Congressional District 08. Submitted at Washington D.C. March 6, 2014. https://www.gsa.gov/cdnstatic/FY2015_New_York_NY_Ted_Weiss_Federal_Building_17.pdf.

Protecting Public Health in New York City. New York State Department of Health and Human Hygiene. April 2005. https://www1.nyc.gov/assets/doh/downloads/pdf/bicentennial/historical-booklet.pdf.

Public Law 97-248 Tax Equity and Fiscal Responsibility Act of 1982. 97th Congress of the United States. Passed September 3, 1982.

Records of the Colony of New Plymouth in New England. Court Orders: Vol. 1. 1633–1640. Edited by Nathaniel B. Shurtleff. Boston: Press of William White, 1855.

"Risk Evaluation for Formaldehyde." Environmental Protection Agency. Docket EPA-HQ-OPPT-2018-0438. Initiated December 2019. https://www.epa.gov/assessing-and-managing-chemicals-under-tsca/risk-evaluation-formaldehyde.

"St. Anne's Church Graveyard, LP-0101." Landmarks Preservation Commission. 1967. http://s-media.nyc.gov/agencies/lpc/lp/0101.pdf.

The Second Constitution of the State of New York, 1821. https://www.nycourts.gov/history/legal-history-new-york/documents/Publications_1821-NY-Constitution.pdf.

Senate Bill S3685: Establishes the New York End of Life Options Act. The New York State Senate, 2015–16 Legislative Session.

Slocum, Joshua. "Death with Dignity? A Report on SCI/Dignity Memorial High Prices and Refusal to Disclose These Prices." *Consumer Federation of America*, March 2017. https://funerals.org/wp-content/uploads/2017/03/3-6-17-Funeral-SCI_Report.pdf.

"Triborough Bridge and Tunnel Authority: Triborough Bridge Rehabilitation Project, Randall's and Ward's Island, Manhattan, Phase 1 Archaeological Assessment Report." Prepared by Celia J. Bergoffen. March 8, 2001. http://s-media.nyc.gov/agencies/lpc/arch_reports/287.pdf.

Troy Leon Gregg, Petitioner v. State of Georgia. Argued March 31, 1976, Decided July 2, 1976. (428 US 153; 96 S.Ct. 2909; 49 L.Ed. 2d 859).

"Tweed Courthouse Archeological Survey and Data Retrieval Investigations." Prepared by Hartgen Archaeological Associates Inc., 2003. http://s-media.nyc.gov/agencies/lpc/arch_reports/365_A.pdf.

"Unified Victim Identification System." Louis Sell, Project Manager. The City of New York, Office of the Chief Medical Examiner. 2009. http://www.nyc.gov/html/ocme/downloads/pdf/Special%20Operations/UVIS%20Information%20Guide_20090917.pdf.

"The Union of Utrecht." January 23, 1579. https://constitution.org/1-Constitution/cons/dutch/Union_Utrecht_1579.html.

Washington State Legislature Initiative SB:5001: Concerning Human Remains. Washington State Congress 2019–20. Passed May 1, 2020.

Whitehead, J. Gordon. "The Sworn Affidavit of J. Gordon Whitehead, in the Matter of the Estate of Harry Houdini against the New York Life Insurance Company." March 16, 1927.

William Henry Furman, Petitioner v. State of Georgia. Argued January 17, 1972, Decided June 29, 1972. (408 US 238; 92 S.Ct. 2726; 33 L.Ed.2d 346).

Zavin, Shirley. "Designation List 177, LP-1408: New York City Farm Colony-Seaview Hospital Historic District." Landmarks Preservation Commission. 1985. http://s-media.nyc.gov/agencies/lpc/lp/1408.pdf.

——— "Designation List 178, LP-1399: Rossville A.M.E Zion Church Cemetery." Landmarks Preservation Commission. 1985. http://s-media.nyc.gov/agencies/lpc/lp/1399.pdf.

Websites

Adair, Carl. "History." Zion Episcopal Church. Last updated October 3, 2019. https://zionepiscopal.org/about-us/history/.

Adams, Michael Henry. "Harlem's St. Nicholas Place and the Remarkable Rebirth of the Bailey-Blake-Spollen House!" August 1, 2012. https://mrmhadams.typepad.com/blog/2012/08/my-entry.html.

"African Burial Ground in Elmhurst, 1828-?" Historic District Council. Updated November 28, 2018. https://hdc.org/policy/landmark-the-elmhurst-african-burial-ground/.

The Alice Austen House Museum. https://aliceausten.org/.

American Civil War Institute. "New York in the Civil War." September 3, 2013. http://americancivilwarinstitute.blogspot.com/2013/09/new-york-in-civil-war.html.

American Medical Association. "Physician Assisted Suicide." https://www.ama-assn.org/delivering-care/ethics/physician-assisted-suicide.

Archives of the Mayor's Press Office. "Mayor Giuliani Signs Bill That Adds The Name 'Walter Jonas Judah Street' To Section of St. James Place." October 18, 1999. http://www.nyc.gov/html/om/html/99b/pr416-99.html.

ArchNY. "Burials in Our Catholic Cemeteries." Archdiocese of New York. March 2, 2017. https://archny.org/burials-in-our-catholic-cemeteries/.

Art of Dying Institute. https://www.artofdying.org/.

Audubon Park Alliance. "A Walk through the Audubon Park Historic District." http://www.audubonparkny.com/AudubonParkTrinityCemeteryTour.html.

Basilica of St. Patrick's Old Cathedral. https://oldcathedral.org/.

Bok, Leon. "Dutch Burial Grounds in America: History and Survival." Dodenakkers. April 9, 2010. https://www.dodenakkers.nl/artikelen-overzicht/foreign-section/north-america/dutch-burial-grounds-in-america-history-and-survival.html.

The Bowery Boys. https://www.boweryboyshistory.com/.

Calvary Cemetery. https://calvarycemeteryqueens.com/.

Catholic Cemeteries of the Roman Catholic Diocese of Brooklyn. https://www.ccbklyn.org/.

Cayuga Museum of History and Art. http://cayugamuseum.org/.

Celestis Memorial Space Flights. https://www.celestis.com/.

Cemetery Records Online. http://www.interment.net/Default.htm.

Central Park Conservancy. "The Rediscovery and Research of Seneca Village." November 25, 2019. https://www.centralparknyc.org/articles/rediscovery-and-research-of-seneca-village.

The Church of Saint Luke in the Fields. https://stlukeinthefields.org/about-us/history/.

Church of St. Raymond. "Sales and Pricing." https://straymondparish.org/sales-and-pricing.

Clark, David. "Cicely Saunders, the 1960s, and the USA." University of Glasgow, End of Life Studies. July 21, 2014. http://endoflifestudies.academicblogs.co.uk/cicely-saunders-the-1960s-and-the-usa/.

Cobb, Geoffrey Owen. "Paderewski's Heart in Greenpoint." Historic Greenpoint. February 18, 2015. https://historicgreenpoint.wordpress.com/2015/02/18/paderewski-heart-in-greenpoint/.

Columbia University DeathLAB. http://deathlab.org/.

Commonwealth Institute of Funeral Service. http://commonwealth.edu/about/history/.

Congregation Rodeph Sholom. https://rodephsholom.org/.

Congregation Shearith Israel. https://shearithisrael.org/.

The Coroners' Society of England and Wales. https://www.coronersociety. org.uk/the-coroners-society/history/.

Cox, John. "Houdini Lying in State at Elks Lodge #1." Wild About Harry. May 24, 2014. https://www.wildabouthoudini.com/2014/05/houdini-lying-in-state-at-elks-lodge-1.html.

Cremation Ink. https://cremationink.com/.

"Cremation Urns, Headstones, Caskets, Memorials, Cremation Jewelry." Memorials.com.

Death Penalty Information Center. 2021. https://deathpenaltyinfo.org/state-and-federal-info/federal-death-penalty.

Department of State, Division of Cemeteries. https://www.dos.ny.gov/cmty/index.html.

De Vries, Hubert. "The Christogram, Symbol of Armed Authority." National Arms and Emblems, Past and Present. March 3, 2014. http://www.hubert-herald.nl/Christogram.htm.

Dignity Memorial. https://www.dignitymemorial.com.

Donate Life Registry. https://donatelife.ny.gov/about-donation/.

Ellenberger, Allan R. "Toto the Story of a Dog." *Hollywoodland*. June 15, 2011. http://allanellenberger.com/tag/ventura-freeway/.

Erenow. https://erenow.net/.

Eternal Reefs. https://www.eternalreefs.com/.

FASCI (Friends of Abandoned Cemeteries, Inc. Staten Island). http://richmond.nygenweb.net/facsi/index.html.

FEMA. "COVID-19 Funeral Assistance." Last updated April 21, 2021. https://www.fema.gov/disasters/coronavirus/economic/funeral-assistance.

Ferncliff Cemetery. https://ferncliffcemetery.com/.

Final Arrangements Network. https://www.finalarrangementsnetwork.com/.

Find a Grave. https://www.findagrave.com/.

Fordham University. https://www.fordham.edu/.

Forever Legacy Eternal Mausoleums. https://www.mausoleums.com/.

Foundation for the Advancement of Sephardic Studies and Culture. "Jonas Judah: The First American-born Jew to Enroll in Medical School." http://www.sephardicstudies.org/judah.html.

French Church du Saint-Esprit. https://stesprit.org/about-us/.

French, Mary. "New York City Cemetery Project." https://nycemtery.wordpress.com.

Fresh Pond Crematory. http://www.freshpondcrematory.com/content/About_Cremation_FAQ.htm.

Genealogy Addict. "Capt. John Underhill." My Genealogy Addiction. https://www.mygenealogyaddiction.com/Ancestors/Capt.-John-Underhill.

Geni. "Capt. John Underhill." Last updated December 30, 2020. https://www.geni.com/people/Capt-John-Underhill/6000000000387506388?through=6000000003649083065.

———. "Sir Robert Lawrence." Last updated September 24, 2017. https://www.geni.com/people/Sir-Robert-Lawrence/6000000003826226307.

Giardino, Neil. "The Traditions of Palo Mayombe." *Pavement Pieces*. May 13, 2015. https://pavementpieces.com/traditions-of-palo-mayombe/.

Gibson, Christine. "A Little History." Elks USA. https://www.elks.org/lodges/LodgePages.cfm?LodgeNumber=2726&ID=7882.

Gonzàlez-Rivera, Christian, Jonathan Bowels and Eli Dvorkin. "New York's Older Adult Population Is Booming Statewide." Center for and Urban Future. February 2019. https://nycfuture.org/research/new-yorks-older-adult-population-is-booming-statewide.

Grant Monument Association. https://grantstomb.org/.

Green-Wood Cemetery. "Full Price List." 2021. https://www.green-wood.com/full-price-list/.

———. "Green Burial." 2021. https://www.green-wood.com/burial/.

Grove Street Cemetery. https://www.grovestreetcemetery.org/.

Hartsdale Pet Cemetery. https://petcem.com/.

Health Resources and Services Administration. "Organ Donor Statistics." Last reviewed April 2021. https://www.organdonor.gov/statistics-stories/statistics.html.

Heavenly Stars Fireworks. https://heavenlystarsfireworks.com/.

Hebrew Free Burial Association. https://www.hebrewfreeburial.org/.

Holy Smoke LLC. http://www.myholysmoke.com/.

India's British Cemeteries. "Nicholas Morse." November 3, 2015. https://indiasbritishcemeteries.wordpress.com/2015/11/03/nicholas-morse/.

International Association of Jewish Genealogical Societies. "International Jewish Cemetery Project." https://iajgscemetery.org/usa/new-york-ny/.

The Irvington Woods. "Hermit's Grave." https://www.theirvingtonwoods.org/hermits-grave/.

Kingsbridge Historical Society (Documents compiled by Nick Dembrowski). "The Kingsbridge Burial Grounds in Van Cortlandt Park." https://kingsbridgehistoricalsociety.org/kingsbridge-burial-grounds-within-van-cortlandt-park/.

Knights of Columbus. https://www.kofc.org/en/todays-knights/history/ 1882-1899.html.

Library of Congress. "Immigration and Relocation in U.S. History: The Great Arrival." https://www.loc.gov/classroom-materials/immigration/ italian/the-great-arrival/.

MacMillan, Alex Frew. "Learning Lessons from the Grave: The Remains of Chinese Emigrants Produced a Paper Trail of the Modern Chinese World." The Chinese University of Hong Kong. August 2015. https:// www.cuhk.edu.hk/english/features/professor-yip-hon-ming.html.

Mafia Hitters. https://mafiahitters.com/.

The Marshall Project. https://www.themarshallproject.org/.

Mayo Clinic. https://mayoclinic.org.

McRay, Greg. "Death and Taxes: Understanding 501(c)(13) Cemetery Companies." Foundation Group. May 7, 2019. https://www.501c3.org/ death-and-taxes-understanding-501c13-cemetery-companies/.

Miller, Francesca. "American Resurrection: The Doctors' Riot of 1788." Dirty, Sexy History. July 7, 2016. https://dirtysexyhistory.com/2016/07/07/ american-resurrection-the-doctors-riot-of-1788/.

Morbid Anatomy. https://www.morbidanatomy.org/.

Mount Auburn Cemetery. https://mountauburn.org/?cache.

Mount Lebanon Cemetery. https://www.mountlebanoncemetery.com/.

National Association for Homecare and Hospice. https://www.nahc.org/.

National Center for Biotechnology Information. https://www.ncbi.nlm.nih.gov/.

National Funeral Directors Association. https://portal.nfda.org/Resource-Store.

National Hospice and Palliative Care Organization. https://www.nhpco.org/.

The National Museum of the American Indian. https://www.si.edu/ newsdesk/factsheets/national-museum-american-indian-new-york.

National Museum of Funeral History. https://www.nmfh.org/.

National Park Service. https://www.nps.gov/index.htm.

Naval History and Heritage Command. "Famous Navy Quotations." August 19, 1019. https://www.history.navy.mil/browse-by-topic/heritage/famous-navy-quotations.html.

The New Haven Preservation Trust. http://nhpt.org/.

The New York Academy of Medicine. https://nyamcenterforhistory.org/.

New York City Council. https://council.nyc.gov/.

New York City Department of City Planning. "Population-NYC Population." https://www1.nyc.gov/site/planning/planning-level/nyc-population/ population-facts.page.

New York City Marble Cemetery. https://www.nycmc.org/.

New York City Parks Department. https://www.nycgovparks.org/.

New York Correction History Society. http://correctionhistory.org/.

New York Department of State. "Cemeteries." https://dos.ny.gov/cemeteries.

New-York Historical Society. "Seneca Village and the Making of Central Park." https://www.nyhistory.org/seneca/village5.html.

New York Landmarks Conservancy. https://nylandmarks.org/.

New York Marble Cemetery. https://marblecemetery.org/.

New York State Association of Cemeteries. http://nysac.com/.

New York State Unified Court System. http://nycourts.gov/.

NOLO. https://nolo.com.

NYCEDC. "126th Street African Burial Ground Memorial and Mixed-Use Project." 2019. https://edc.nyc/project/east-126th-harlem-african-burial-ground-project.

NYPD Shomrim Society. https://www.nypdshomrim.org/.

Officer Down Memorial Page. https://www.odmp.org/.

The Order of the Good Death. http://www.orderofthegooddeath.com/.

Plaza Jewish Community Chapel Inc. "The Cost Advantage of Plaza." https://www.plazajewishcommunitychapel.org/cost-comparision/.

Recompose. https://recompose.life/who-we-are/.

Rohatyn Jewish Heritage. "Jewish Traditions for Death, Burial, and Mourning." https://rohatynjewishheritage.org/en/culture/death-burial-mourning/.

St. James Cathedral Basilica. https://brooklyncathedral.org/history.

St. Peter's Church-Our Lady of the Rosary. https://spcolr.org/.

Sandy Ground Historical Society. https://sandyground.wordpress.com.

Schmidt, Barbara. "*The New York Times* Obituaries for Blind Tom." Twainquotes.com. http://www.twainquotes.com/TomObit.html.

————— "Where Is Blind Tom Buried?" Twainquotes.com. http://www.twainquotes.com/archangelsmystery.html.

Seneca Village Project. http://projects.mcah.columbia.edu/seneca_village/.

Service Corporation International. https://www.sci-corp.com/.

Sharpe, William. "A Pig Upon the Town: Charles Dickens in New York." September 22, 1996. https://www.thefreelibrary.com/A+pig+upon+the+town%3A+Charles+Dickens+in+New+York.-a0188966630.

Simmons, Josh. "Walk on Water." eCatholic. 2021. https://ecatholic.com/blog/walk-on-water.

Spady, Matthew. "100 Years of Tradition: The Church of the Intercession Celebrates Clement Clarke Moore." Audubon Park Perspectives. December 11, 2011. https://audubonparkperspectives.org/2011/12/11/101-years-of-tradition-the-church-of-the-intercession-celebrates-clement-clarke-moore/.

The Spring Street Archaeological Project. https://springstreetarchaeology. syr.edu/.

Statista Business Data Platform. https://www.statista.com/.

Temple Shaaray Tefila. https://shaaraytefilanyc.org/.

The Theosophical Society in America. "Up in Smoke: Theosophy and the Revival of Cremation." 2009. https://www.theosophical.org/ publications/quest-magazine/1684-up-in-smoke-theosophy-and-the-revival-of-cremation.

Trinity Church Wall Street. "The General and the Monument." September 19, 2011. https://trinitywallstreet.org/stories-news/general-and-monument.

———. "History of Trinity Church Wall Street." https://trinitywallstreet. org/history.

———. "Unearthing Our Past." February 4, 2004. https://trinitywallstreet. org/stories-news/unearthing-our-past.

U.S. Department of Veterans' Affairs, National Cemetery Administration. Last updated April 29, 2021. https://www.cem.va.gov/.

USGenWebArchives. "Famous Families of New York, published 1917." http://files.usgwarchives.net/ny/state/bios/ffny/lawrence.txt.

Woodlawn Cemetery. https://www.woodlawn.org/.

World Population Review. "Civil War Casualties by State 2021." https:// worldpopulationreview.com/state-rankings/civil-war-casualties-by-state.

Miscellaneous

Congregation B'Nai Tikvah Beth Israel. "Guide to Jewish Cemetery." 2016. https://www.cbtbi.org/wp-content/uploads/2016/10/Guide-to-Jewish-Cemetery.pdf.

Forman, Adam. "Caution Ahead: Overdue Investments for New York's Aging Infrastructure." Edited by Jonathan Bowles and David Giles. Center for an Urban Future, Reporting Publication. March 2014. https://files. eric.ed.gov/fulltext/ED555648.pdf.

Juet, Robert. "Juet's Journal of Hudson's 1609 Voyage," from the 1625 edition of *Purchas His Pilgrimes*. Transcribed by Brea Barthel. New Netherland Museum/Half Moon. 2006.

"Lauren's Law in New York Becomes Permanent, Focuses on Organ Donations." Allison Dunne. Radio Broadcast on October 18, 2017, on WAMC, Northeast Public Radio: *Midday Magazine*. https://www.wamc. org/post/laurens-law-ny-becomes-permanent-focuses-organ-donations.

Lazarus, Emma. "The New Colossus." 1883.

Morrisey, Mary Beth, David Leven and Thomas Caprio. "Palliative Care in New York State." Collaborative for Palliative Care, in collaboration with End of Life Choices, New York, and Finger Lakes Geriatric Education Center as the University of Rochester. 2017. http://endoflifechoicesny.org/wp-content/uploads/2017/07/PalliativeCareBooklet7-24-17.pdf.

"Nimoy Explains Origin of Vulcan Greeting." Yiddish Book Project. *New York Times* video. February 27, 2015. https://www.nytimes.com/video/obituaries/100000003536154/nimoy-explains-origin-of-vulcan-greeting.html.

Olcott, Henry Steel. "Old Diary Leaves. First Series, 1874–78." Minh Triêt Thiêng Liêng. https://www.minhtrietmoi.org/Theosophy/Olcott/OLD%20DIARY%20LEAVES%201.htm#_Toc367364966.

Secrets of the Dead: The Woman in the Iron Coffin. Directed by Adam Luria, produced by Stephanie Carter. Aired October 3, 2018, on PBS.

"60 Minutes Investigates the Death of Jeffrey Epstein (transcript)." Produced by Oriana Zill de Granados. Aired on January 5, 2020 on CBS. https://www.cbsnews.com/news/did-jeffrey-epstein-kill-himself-60-minutes-investigates-2020-01-05/.

ABOUT THE AUTHOR

K. Krombie has written numerous articles for media outlets in America and the United Kingdom, in addition to film and New York theater reviews. A longtime obsessive of all things New York City, it's only right that this author lives here now.

Visit us at
www.historypress.com